THE APPIN MURDER

MURDER

The Killing of the Red Fox

SEAMUS CARNEY

'Is't Known who did this more than bloody deed?'
Macbeth

BIRLINN

This edition first published in 2011 by
Birlinn Limited
West Newington House
10 Newington Road
Edinburgh
EH9 1QS

www.birlinn.co.uk

ISBN 978 1 841 58981 7

British Library Cataloguing-in-Publication Data
A catalogue record for this book is available
from the British Library

Typeset by Hewer Text, Edinburgh
Printed and bound in Great Britain by
CPI Antony Rowe, Chippenham, Wiltshire

CONTENTS

List of Illustrations

PREFACE

I am grateful to my old friend Eamon Quinn for his encourage-
ment and suggestions during the writing of this book. I am also
indebted to Colonel RMT Campbell-Preston of Ardchattan
OBE, MC, TD, DL for permitting me to read relevant letters
from his family archives and for allowing into print for the first
time the letter from his ancestor, Alexander Campbell of
Ardchattan.

All sums mentioned in the text are in pounds sterling.
Place-names are spelt as in current Ordnance Survey maps with
the single exception of Fassiefern, which in the eighteenth
century and in later years seems to have been universally
accorded three syllables. With apologies to Scottish scholars I
have taken minor liberties with the names of two of the central
characters to avoid confusing English and other readers unfamil-
iar with so many similar appellations.

My thanks are extended to the staffs of the following libraries
and centres of information for their generous assistance: Inver-
ness Library, Inverness; The West Highland Museum, Fort
William; Scottish Record Office, HM General Register House,
Edinburgh; National Library of Scotland, Edinburgh; Central
Library, Edinburgh; Court of the Lord Lyon, HM New Register
House, Edinburgh; Central Library, Birmingham; Public Record
Offices (Chancery Lane and Kew Gardens), London; South
Eastern Divisional Library, Worthing; Service Historique de
l'Armée de Terre, Château de Vincennes, Paris; Ministère de la
Culture et de la Communication, Paris; New York State
Historical Association, Cooperstown, USA.

Seamus Carney

The Main Characters in 1752

Cameron, Archibald, 22, nephew of laird of Fasnacloich

Cameron, John, laird of Fassiefern, acting leader of Clan Cameron in Scotland, uncle of exiled Chief John Cameron of Lochiel

Campbell, Archibald, 70, 3rd Duke of Argyll, Lord Justice General of Scotland

Campbell, Archibald of Stonefield, 56, Advocate, Sheriff-Depute of Argyll

Campbell, Colin, 44?, laird of Glenure, Crown factor on forfeited estates of Ardsheal, Callert and part of Lochiel

Campbell, Donald, 47, laird of Airds, Justice of the Peace, landlord of James Stewart in Aucharn

Campbell, Duncan, 36, brother of Glenure, Sheriff-Substitute of Perthshire

Campbell, Janet, (née Mackay), 21?, wife of Colin of Glenure, niece of Lord Reay

Campbell, John, 56, 3rd Earl of Breadalbane

Campbell, John, 52, laird of Barcaldine, half-brother of Glenure, Crown factor on the forfeited estate of Perth

Campbell, Mungo, 24, solicitor, natural son of John Campbell of Barcaldine

Crawfurd, John, 30, Lieutenant-colonel, Pulteney's Regiment, officer commanding Fort William

Drummond, James 'More' Macgregor, son of Rob Roy Macgregor

Erskine, Charles, 72, Lord Tinwald, Lord Justice-Clerk

Fraser, Simon, 26, advocate, formerly Master of Lovat

Grant, William of Prestongrange, 51, Lord Advocate of Scotland

Maccoll, Dugald, 24, servant of James Stewart in Aucharn

Maccoll, Ewan, ('Red Ewan'), smallholder, brother of John Don

Maccoll, John 'Beg', 27, servant of James Stewart in Aucharn

Maccoll, John 'Don' or 'Breck', 40, stockman to the laird of Appin

Maccoll, John 'More', 37, servant of James Stewart in Aucharn

Maccoll, Katharine, 16, dairymaid of James Stewart in Aucharn

Maclaren, Colin, 22, merchant in Stirling

Pelham, Henry, 56, First Commissioner of the Treasury, Chancellor of the Exchequer

Stewart, Alexander, 68, laird of Ballachulish

Stewart, Alexander of Edinglassie, solicitor to James Stewart in Aucharn

Stewart, Alexander, ('Sandy Bane'), 30, pedlar, cousin of Allan Breck Stewart and friend of James Stewart in Aucharn

Stewart, Allan 'Beg' or 'Oig', elder son of James Stewart in Aucharn

Stewart, Allan 'Breck', 30, foster-son of James Stewart in Aucharn, private soldier in Ogilvy's Regiment in the French army

Stewart, Charles, 38, notary in Maryburgh

Stewart, Charles, younger son of James Stewart in Aucharn

Stewart, Donald, 30, nephew and son-in-law of laird of Ballachulish

Stewart, Dugald, 10th chief of Appin Stewarts, Baron Appin in the Jacobite Peerage

Stewart, James, 57?, tacksman in Aucharn, illegitimate half-brother of attainted laird of Ardsheal

Stewart, James, 29, eldest son of laird of Fasnacloich. Probable company captain in Appin Regiment in 1745

Stewart, John, 26, eldest surviving son of laird of Ballachulish

Stewart, Margaret, wife of James Stewart in Aucharn

Stewart, William, 36, merchant in Maryburgh, cousin and brother-in-law of James Stewart in Aucharn

1 Red Colin Dies

FOUR MEN, strung out in a lengthy line, picked their way along the narrow, rocky track through the wood of Lettermore. Below them and to their right, the blue waters of Loch Linnhe gleamed through occasional gaps in birch and conifer. Flanking the old bridleway on the other side, the hill rose steeply in a tumble of mossy boulders, bushes and stunted trees. The leading wayfarer was on foot, the others on horseback. The middle rider, Colin Campbell of Glenure, held the post of Crown factor, or land-agent, for the estate through which he was travelling. A red-haired man in his mid forties, he was on his way to evict several tenants on the morrow, 15 May 1752. The time was around half-past five in the afternoon.

A single shot cracked the silence. Two musket-balls pierced Glenure's back. He shouted: 'Oh, I am dead. He's going to shoot you. Take care of yourself', or words of that import. About forty yards ahead his nephew Mungo reined sharply, then dismounted and rushed back to help the stricken factor, who still remained in the saddle, frequently moaning, 'I am dead.' Two events then occurred of whose sequence the young man could not afterwards be certain. He assisted his uncle off his horse and laid him on the ground, and started up the hill a few paces in search of the assassin. He saw – as he was to state formally a few days later – a man in a short coat and breeches, both dun in colour, fleeing up the brae. The runner carried a gun but was at so great a distance that Mungo was convinced he could not have fired the shot. Donald Kennedy, who had led the party on foot, heard the report, followed by a cry of horror. He ran back and found Glenure on the blood-stained ground. Mungo had unbuttoned the dying man's waistcoat and Kennedy saw a hole in the shirt made by an emerging ball. They were quickly joined by John Mackenzie, the victim's servant, who had heard the shot but thought nothing of it. Mungo ordered him to mount

1

the best horse and ride the two miles to the Kentallen Inn, where he might find some of Glenure's kinsmen. The factor had been due to meet them there that evening. The servant was to bring them back immediately. Mackenzie galloped off. Shortly after his departure, close to six o'clock, Glenure died. Mungo urged Kennedy to hurry to Ballachulish House, not more than a quarter of an hour's brisk walk away, and fetch the laird and his people. Though reluctant to leave the young man alone and defenceless, Kennedy set off.

Glenure's murder was not only to create an abiding mystery, but also result in a controversial trial and inspire two of Robert Louis Stevenson's greatest novels. Its roots lay in the rebellion of 1745, when Prince Charles Edward's army, after a spectacular campaign that took it as far as Derby, was finally destroyed at Culloden. The victors, resolute to stamp out Scottish insurrections once and for all, launched a programme of pacification, starting by killing off the rebels left wounded on the battlefield. Redcoat bands ravaged the glens, burning, rustling and looting. Crofters fled their homes to the hills, where some perished in the raw winter of 1746. On one raid the marauders turned a woman and her young children out of the house after thoughtfully shooting the family cat lest it should provide a source of food. One hundred and twenty rebels were executed, and some of their heads grimaced aloft on city gates to warn dissidents against resisting the advance of civilisation. The Government weighed in with a spate of legislation, mostly punitive. The estates of rebel leaders were declared forfeit to the Crown. Clan chiefs and landowners were deprived of their heritable jurisdictions, that is, the right to try their own people and levy what amounted to private armies. There were to be no more petty kings. The Episcopal Church, seen by London as a nursery of sedition, suffered penal restrictions designed to kill it off. Amnesty was granted to all who had taken up arms except eighty uncaptured notables and the Macgregors, who were deemed to be incorrigible. A Disarming Act required all civilians living north of the Highland Line to surrender their weapons. Failure to do so by 1 August 1747 carried a penalty of a fifteen pound fine which, if left unpaid for a month, could be upgraded to transportation or imprisonment. The Act also banned the kilt, trews, tartan cloth and all other accessories of Highland dress, a prohibition intended to snuff out the rebellious spirit of which the vivid garb was held to be the outward expression. Not until the Scots were indistinguishable from their southern neighbours would the United Kingdom become a united kingdom.

Survivors of the Jacobite army straggled back to their glens and set about picking up the severed threads of their lives. They repaired the drystone walls of their dwellings and rethatched roofs burned off by incendiarists. Those with a few pounds to spare bought livestock to replace animals driven away or shot. Slowly life returned to normal, but normality for most people meant an existence scratched out near the starvation line. An archaic and Byzantine system of land tenure had endlessly subdivided arable tracts into strips too tiny for economic cultivation. In 1749 factors took up office as managers of the forfeited estates. They were Highlanders recruited from the clans that had remained loyal to the Government, and most had been in arms against the Prince. They were hated with that special fervour which subject peoples have always reserved for satraps of their own race, so as Mungo watched Glenure breathe his last on that woodland path the atrocity, though it horrified him to his depths, cannot have come as an unthinkable eventuality.

For an hour and a half he stood guardian over his uncle's corpse. Light was failing. He was a solitary unarmed Campbell in Stewart country, at a time when the two clans were at pistol-point. The proposed evictions had whipped up widespread resentment. Guns, in defiance of the official ban, were openly on display in many an outhouse. At any moment the assassin, or assassins, might return to double the gory tally. Footsteps approached from the direction of Kentallen and a woman came into view. Mungo asked her to stay with him

3

until help arrived but she refused and passed on. His relief must have been intense when Kennedy appeared with Stewart of Ballachulish and some of his family and tenants. But this feeling was tinged with a harsher emotion. In a letter written shortly afterwards he contended that there was not one of those people who would have grieved if he had shared his uncle's fate.

In the meantime Mackenzie's ride to the Kentallen Inn had drawn a blank, for Glenure's prospective guests, Campbell of Ballieveolan and his sons, had not yet arrived. He spurred on to Glen Duror, where Ballieveolan rented a farm. He met one of his quarry's tenants who advised him to call at the house of James Stewart, a man who was likely to know the whereabouts of Ballieveolan. The weeping Mackenzie pressed his mount the brief distance to James's farm and broke the news. 'Lord bless me, was he shot?' exclaimed James – a reaction that was to be recalled during his trial for complicity in the murder. The farmer went on to express his shock at the outrage. As Mackenzie told it, he 'wrung his hands, express'd great concern at what had happened, as what might bring innocent people to trouble, and pray'd that innocent people might not be brought to trouble.' Mackenzie asked him to go and look after the corpse and James consented. He said he knew nothing of Ballieveolan's current location but gave the lad directions to his house. Mackenzie rode off but found the rising ground gruelling for his horse. He persuaded a man he met to walk to Ballieveolan's home a little way up the glen and send him to the murder scene. Then he sped back to the wood, where Mungo and the Ballachulish villagers stood around the corpse.

The dead man had been born about 1708, the second son of a comparatively wealthy landowner. On the death of his father he inherited property in Glen Ure and lived the life of a gentleman farmer, punctuated by trips to Edinburgh for business and pleasure. To his amorous nature he gave full rein in dalliance with the ladies, four of whom bore him daughters. During the 'Forty-five he served against the rebels as a militia

4

captain. In March 1746 Glenure was joint commander of a force posted on the Atholl Braes to prevent a westward foray by the retreating insurgents. He confided to a senior clansman that his position was impregnable to a daylight attack but could be overrun by night. Next day he left the garrison in order to conduct some official business and used the occasion to visit his half-brother. He stayed the night and woke to the news that the garrison had been swamped by a surprise assault in the hours of darkness. By a woeful coincidence his fellow commander had also been absent from his post on a military errand. The resulting commotion echoed through the army, and a searing report reached the desk of the Secretary-General. A courtmartial seemed inevitable, and Glenure was shunted out of harm's way as an aide-de-camp to the commanding general in the east. It was probably the rout of Charles Edward's army a month later that saved him from a tribunal. In the afterglow of victory disciplinary proposals were dropped, but he and his colleague were reprimanded, and his stock must have sunk in the eyes of the clan leaders. Loudon's Regiment, in which he held a lieutenant's commission, saw action in Flanders in the years after the rebellion, and he is said to have acquitted himself with credit there.

When the Rising collapsed the Government took the decision to conduct an organised survey of Scotland. The unmapped state of the Highlands was creating difficulties both for the military authorities and the planners who were preparing to appoint factors to the lands of attainted rebels. Few of these properties were rigorously documented as to their extent, or even ownership. Much territory had been acquired at a remote period when warlords preferred to define their borders with the edge of the sword, rather than the scratch of a quill. The Barons of the Exchequer of Scotland were assigned the duty of administering the forfeited estates, and by the summer of 1747 factors had been nominated, one of whom was Colin Campbell of Glenure. Then a memorial questioning the suitability of some of the factors arrived in Whitehall. It came to the attention of Henry Pelham, First Commissioner of the Treasury and, in effect, Prime Minister. Alarmed, Pelham dictated a Treasury minute: 'Write to the Barons of the Exheq: of Scotland that the Lords of the Treary (sic) have Suspended the Approbation of the Factors for the Forfeited Estates there till they have had their opinion upon some Hints contained in a Mem[1] presented to their Lordships upon the subject of those Factors. Send also with the Letter an Extract of the said Hints.' Little is known of this incident beyond the fact that it took place; no surviving document names the suspect factors. Almost certainly Glenure was one of the nominees whose fitness for the office was called in doubt. He was viewed with misgivings on account of his blood ties with the Camerons, the most implacable of the Jacobite clans. His mother was the daughter of one of their clan chiefs and the aunt of another, the 'Gentle' Lochiel who led his people out when Prince Charles landed. This check to the smooth installation of the factors sprang from Whitehall's fear and suspicion of the Scots; the advance to Derby was too recent to permit anything but the most scrupulous screening of Crown servants. There ensued a hiatus of six months, devoted perhaps to the investigation of the hints. In March of 1748 the nominated factors were confirmed in their posts and early in the next year Glenure received his commission. Soon afterwards he married a well-connected teenage girl and settled down in his modern, sprawling house.

The question of why he sought the factorship has provoked differing answers. His own explanation was that he liked to keep busy. As well as managing his property he was active as a member of the Commissioners of Supply for Argyll, a kind of proto- County Council which dealt with the public works of the shire. It has been written, with no contributory evidence, that he saw the post as the next rung in his climb to higher honours and rewards. Certainly it was not the lavishness of the salary that beguiled him; his annual stipend was ten pounds, ten shillings and seven pence halfpenny. More than probably his motives blended public duty and personal advantage in a proportion not even he could assess. His stewardship embraced the Cameron estates of Callert and part of Lochiel, and the Stewart property of Ardsheal, where he met his end.

The lands of Ardsheal lay at the north end of the district of Appin, near the confluence of the lochs Linnhe and Leven. When Glenure took office the estate was being administered by the James Stewart to whose farm John Mackenzie rode after the murder. James was a small man whose age may be guessed as somewhere between forty-seven and fifty-four. Born a natural son of the fourth laird of Ardsheal, his education was carried to a stage where he could speak and write fluent English – not a commonplace accomplishment in the Gaelic-speaking Highlands. At his trial it was to be alleged that he took part in the rebellion of 1719, but this he later denied. Before the 'Forty-five he held the tenancy of a farm at Auchindarroch, a village a mile or so up Glen Duror, from his half-brother Charles, the laird. James was the tacksman for the estate, 'tack' being a Scots term for a lease. Highland landowners found it profitable and convenient to lease spacious tracts to responsible agents, who were usually close relatives. These agents, or tacksmen, in turn sublet the lands in smaller units. For reasons unknown Ardsheal evicted his brother.

When the Stuart prince unfurled his standard the Appin Stewarts, led by Ardsheal, joined him. James saw service as a junior officer, the captain of his local company of thirty-five men. When the rebellion crumbled Ardsheal fled to France and James remained at home, making his peace with the Government. He moved back into Auchindarroch with his wife and children, and took up the management of his brother's property. As Ardsheal had left his wife behind, James imposed surcharges, or 'second rents', on the tenants to provide for her and her children. When Glenure was awarded the factorship she left for France to be reunited with her husband. James's authority, although derived initially from his lineage, was soon buttressed by his competence. Not only did he run the farm in fertile Glen Duror but he was a busy dealer, a middleman and small-scale entrepreneur with a dozen irons in the fire. It was to him that the country people turned when baffled by legal and financial problems, and he fostered a succession of orphan children in a far from spacious household. He was known throughout Appin and Lochaber, needing no further identification than 'James of the Glen'. Prosperous by the impoverished standards of the region, he employed at least seven menials. James more than liked a drop of spirits, indulging his enthusiasm to the point of distilling it in an outbuilding set aside for the purpose. By his own reckoning he was related to Glenure, a quite credible claim in view of the frequency of intermarriage among the clan gentry, whatever their political and religious preferences. The two men were further linked by ties of social position, education and wide responsibilities. Their homes lay five miles apart, a fact which made them near neighbours in that sparsely populated area.

As factor, Glenure's early transactions with James were tactful and conciliatory. He made the tacksman his unofficial subagent and empowered him to continue collecting rents and letting properties. He let him know that he had no objection to the additional levy for Lady Ardsheal, 'Lady' being a courtesy title extended to lairds' wives. When the lady bolted to France, Glenure asked the Barons for instructions on how to proceed against her for the recovery of monies due to the Crown. He gave it as his own opinion that the trouble and expense were not worth the candle. His masters disagreed: a legal order must be taken out against her, 'for it may be of use'. Red Colin lodged the claim at Edinburgh. By these gestures Glenure sought to placate the sullen Stewarts, but few of them were yet ready to accept the olive branch. They still smouldered in their sense of outrage that Government troops had swept through Appin in 1746, putting its little villages to the torch and driving off the cattle. Ardsheal

House, a handsome mansion set on a rugged hillside overlooking Loch Linnhe, had been dismantled and its furniture, freestone and slate sold off to enrich the nation's coffers by four hundred pounds. Glenure was soon to sigh that he found himself dealing with a set of people who would do nothing pleasantly or without compulsion.

In the autumn of 1749 the factor, acting on the instructions of the Barons, called for payment of rent arrears dating back to the Rebellion. On behalf of the tenants James sought a restraining injunction, probably protesting that they had already paid the cash to Ardsheal and his wife. The injunction was refused and Glenure summoned a Baron-bailie court to sue for payment. He won his decree and the tenants, one of whom was James, were ordered to make up the deficit. The tacksman defrayed part of the debt by paying about fifty-one pounds. Seven months later the factor demanded settlement of the remainder from eleven tenants, including James. The harassed farmer petitioned for the annulment of the debt on the grounds that the money had gone to the Ardsheals, but his plea cut no ice. The court told the tenants to pay up. The fact that the president and clerk of the assembly bore the Stewart name cannot have made it easier for James to swallow its ruling. He allowed some months to elapse before submitting a second instalment of fifty-one pounds, leaving a small outstanding sum.

While these wrangles cannot have endeared Glenure to James they were not so serious as to effect a final break, and by the spring of 1751 relations between the pair were still civil. Then two incidents may have caused the tacksman to regard Glenure as no longer simply an adversary but an enemy. The latter asked him to vacate his farm, possibly citing the fact that he was still behind with the rent. Knowing resistance to be futile, James complied without waiting for formal notice to quit. He moved half a mile to Aucharn, a farm which lay on the level land at the mouth of the glen. The soil was fruitful and the site in many ways superior to his previous one, but these benefits

9

were outweighed by his banishment from Auchindarroch village, the heart of the community, and the entry of a Campbell in his place. Ballieveolan, Glenure's friend and first cousin once removed, took over the vacant property. The expelled man bore his fate with apparent equanimity, but to a close acquaintance he exposed his true feelings. He was anything but satisfied, his contention being that Ballieveolan had used his influence to have him ejected. Another man was to swear that James told him he would be willing to take a shot at Glenure even if he were so disabled as to have to drag himself to a window. Hard on the heels of this blow came a peremptory letter from the factor by express, or special messenger. '. . . something has occurred that makes it necessary that you do not set (let) any part of Ardshiel, Auchindarroch, or Aucharn, till I see you after my return from Inverary.'

The 'something' that prompted Glenure to expel James from his home and unofficial post arose from a long-standing dispute on the Cameron lands across the loch. From the moment of his appointment the people of Lochiel and Callert had shown themselves to be immutably hostile. Red Colin's kinship, far from winning co-operation, aggravated their resentment, adding the name of traitor to that of overlord. His first cousin, Cameron of Fassiefern, had taken over the management of the Lochiel estate when his brother, the chief, fled to France after the Rising. Fassiefern was a diehard supporter of the House of Stuart who had not taken up arms because he considered the rebellion a crazy enterprise doomed to failure. He was determined not to cede a clan acre to anyone who backed the ruling regime. To such a prickly dissenter all Government officials were anathema, and Glenure was soon to feel the weight of his antagonism. Their first clash came in November, 1749 when the Barons instructed the factor to collect arrears of rent. Some Cameron tenants refused to pay up and Glenure decided to seize their goods in lieu of cash. With a court officer and some of his assistants the angry factor confronted the renters. He reported their response in a letter to his superiors: 'They told the Baron Baillie officer and other servants I sent with, and that in my own presence, That if they dar'd touch or Seize any part of their Effects for payment of his Majesty's Rents they would beat out their brains.' The tenants had been forbidden by Fassiefern to hand over their arrears, by their own admission. Glenure went on to appeal for a military escort when carrying out his duties. The Barons arranged that a squad from Fort William should be available on request, but Glenure never once used it, having later concluded that he was in no danger of attack. Fassiefern was summoned to Edinburgh to explain his conduct. He denied having influenced his people to refuse to pay, and as no one could be found who was willing to sign an affidavit supporting the charge he was released.

Equally ungovernable was the wife of the attainted laird of Callert, Helen Cameron, who had been given a hardship grant of nearly one hundred and seventy pounds after the Rising. Unmollified by this largesse, she insisted on managing her husband's estate, carrying her insolence to the point of felling trees illegally and refusing to disburse rents. Her son was rumoured to be engaged in hiring killers to dispose of Glenure. The story gained sufficient currency to reach the ears of the prospective victim, who did not believe it. Young Callert, not surprisingly, rejected the accusation.

But it was not these difficulties that led Glenure to take the actions which almost certainly inspired his death. His critical quarrel was with John McLauchlan, a cradle Jacobite if his name is anything to go by. During the 'Forty-five he had bought up the cattle of rebels who feared confiscation by the advancing redcoats, and the bargain rate of ten shillings a head netted him a profit quoted as five hundred pounds. In the wake of the Rising he sold meal and brandy to the beaten fugitives in the hills. At the same time he took possession of a farm which had been burned down by Government troops. He rebuilt the house and barns, and when Glenure was appointed told him that he would pay no more than sixteen pounds per annum in rent. Furthermore he would not pay even that amount until he had been reimbursed for his capital outlay. The factor agreed to these conditions without consulting his masters who when they learned about it reprimanded him. Fassiefern sent Glenure a notarised protest at the letting to be forwarded to the Barons. The stage was set for a long and complicated dispute among several protagonists which ultimately affected James of the Glen. The Barons attempted to cut the Gordian knot by ruling that the rental of the farm should be sold to the highest bidder at an auction to be held no later than 15 May 1751, the end of the tenurial year. McLauchlan, faced with possible loss of the farm, was well placed to revenge himself on Glenure if he should be turned out. His father-in-law, the deputy governor of Fort William, had access to the commander-in-chief of the forces in North Britain. He in turn was an authoritative voice in the chambers of Whitehall. There can be little doubt that Glenure, anticipating a complaint from the commander-in-chief to the Secretary of State, removed James Stewart from his home and office to nullify a charge of being 'soft' on Jacobites.

As McLauchlan told it he was prepared to offer thirty-four pounds at the auction but Fassiefern or his friends persuaded him to tender only sixteen pounds. McLauchlan's agent bid that sum and was topped by Fassiefern's representative, who went a pound higher. By this stroke of chicanery Fassiefern acquired the farm but Glenure limited his tenancy to a single year. The commander-in-chief fired off a letter to the appropriate Secretary of State, the Duke of Newcastle, the substance of which was that factors who were Highlanders were bound to favour dissenters, and that everyone who rented land on a forfeited estate should be forced to take an oath of allegiance to the Crown. He enclosed a copy of a letter 'of private intelligence' whose writer he was not at liberty to disclose. It asserted that Jacobites on the districts managed by Glenure now held the best lands at peppercorn rents, and Fassiefern was getting rid of tenants loyal to King George with the full approbation of his cousin. Newcastle showed the

12

report to the king, who instructed him to send it to his brother Pelham for strict investigation. Pelham ordered the Barons not to employ any Highlanders or relatives of the forfeited landowners. In a lengthy reply their Lordships defended Glenure as an eager volunteer in the rebellion, excoriated McLauchlan, whom they plainly believed to have written the letter of private intelligence, and argued that none but a Highlander could carry out a factor's business. Privately they were furious at the result of the auction. They had managed to get rid of McLauchlan, a shady war profiteer, only to burden themselves with the truculent Fassiefern, an irreconcilable opponent of Hanoverian rule. They called Glenure to Edinburgh, severely reprimanded him, decreed that neither Fassiefern nor McLauchlan should have the farm, and gave Glenure a copy of instructions that were to be sent to all factors. Its chief provisions were that no relative or friend of the forfeiting person should be given land, and that only those people who took an oath of allegiance should be allowed to gain leases by public auction.

Through the autumn of 1751 the dispute rumbled on. In November Pelham, warily noting Glenure's blood-relationship with the Camerons, recommended that if suspicions about his loyalty should be proved true he must be dismissed. To anticipate events, the Barons displayed continuing belief in their factor's innocence by renewing his commission in the spring of 1752, and a month before his murder they reported that they had examined the charges thoroughly and found them groundless.

James Stewart must have observed this imbroglio with growing dejection. The arbitrary removal of Fassiefern from a legally procured tenure made it clear that the powers of the Jacobite gentry were as dead as Queen Anne, the last Stuart monarch. At Christmas 1751, some months after his own twofold loss of his home and post as deputy factor, he delivered what sounded like a broad hint to three of his labourers that they should 'take off' the tyrant. However, even then he was on cordial enough terms with Glenure to spend Hogmanay drinking with him at the Kentallen

Inn. The night ended badly. The small party of celebrants did not stint themselves at the bottle and a quarrel broke out between Glenure and an uncle of James's. They lunged to attack each other and John Stewart, the son of the laird of Ballachulish, was obliged to interpose himself more than once between them. He persuaded his two clansmen to leave the hostelry. Once outside, James remembered that he had invited the Campbell to dine at Aucharn next day. He insisted on re-entering to confirm that his guest would fulfil the engagement. This course was sternly vetoed by young Ballachulish, who coaxed the tacksman into remaining outside while he returned to reissue the invitation. He found Glenure standing with a drawn sword in his hand. Ballachulish prevailed on the angry reveller to put his weapon away and drew from him a promise to eat with James. Next morning Glenure presented himself at Aucharn, apologies were exchanged and the meal passed off without incident.

In the spring two fresh vicissitudes afflicted the tacksman. An Act was passed annexing certain forfeited estates inalienably to the Crown. One of these was Ardsheal. This blow was followed by another in late March or early April when Glenure served preliminary eviction notices on five tenants on the attained laird's property. They had been selected with care. All were residents James had introduced before the factor took office and they had no standing leases or right of long-term occupation entitling them to stay. Their tenuous claim to the land they farmed meant that legal obstacles would be few and negotiable. All were up to date with their rents and, as far as is known, they were willing to take the oath of allegiance. Their expulsion was sure to create much wrath in a sept that was noted for its probity. Two years earlier a Government official, sent to the Highlands to survey the clans, had written a report that was almost wholly hostile to the Jacobites. Of the people of Appin he conceded: 'They are not thieves but are industrious in their Business and Honest in their Private Dealings.' Glenure's motive for ousting the occupiers can only have been to silence once and for all the voices that accused him of being a secret sympathiser with the enemies of German George.

Two of those marked down for eviction were tenants of a farm James sublet in Lettermore. One of them was a widow, a fact that doubtless fanned the flame of indignation that flared through Ardsheal and beyond. James at once condemned Glenure's action to his face. The official was unmoved, but probably told the incensed Stewart that he intended to provide employment for the displaced folk with those who would replace them. On 3 April James rode to Edinburgh to apply to the Barons for an order confirming the tenants in their holdings. Unluckily their scheduled session did not take place due to the lack of a quorum and they were not listed to meet until after the date of the evictions. The crusader managed to secure an interview with one of the Barons, who advised him to contrive to stave off the expulsions until the next term when the Barons would see justice done. A protest should be made to Glenure by the threatened Appin and Mamore tenants – for several holders of Cameron leases were also to be removed. James consulted a solicitor who practised before the Court of Session, Scotland's supreme civil court. He recommended that a petition to halt the evictions should be presented to the court. The tacksman did so and was rewarded with a sist, or stay of execution *sine die*. Elated at having gained a vital breathing-space for further legal moves, James saddled up for Appin after an absence of more than three weeks. He engaged Charles Stewart, a kinsman and notary, to act for him in serving the injunction and Stewart summoned to Aucharn the tenants at risk. James and the lawyer explained the position to the three or four who came, stressing that there was no obligation on anyone to join the delegation, but that if they should decide to do so they must conduct themselves peaceably and promise to take the oath. Three tenants chose to form a deputation with the lawyer but James stayed discreetly at home. He told one of his labourers that he would support the tenants as far as the law would allow him. At least two of the supplicants asked Red Colin to permit them to retain their homes. He told them it was too late; the properties had already been let. They then presented the sist. The date was 1 May, precisely two weeks before the statutory term day.

Probably on the next morning Glenure repaired to Edinburgh to take counter-measures. He submitted a plea against the injunction and a Lord of Session rescinded it. James's trial advocates were to claim that through ignorance of legal procedure their client had mistakenly carried away the Bill of Suspension on which he had set out his arguments, with the result that Glenure was ceded the advantage of presenting his case to a different judge against an absent defence. Having won the legal duel the factor recruited the services of Mungo, the twenty-four year old natural son of his half-brother. Mungo was a solicitor, and his presence was intended to ensure that the evictions would be effected in strict accordance with the law. Uncle and nephew rode swiftly north to Glen Ure, alighting there on Saturday, 9 May. On Monday morning they set out for Maryburgh, a village that had grown up beside Fort William, to obtain an ejection order against the Mamore tenants from the sheriff of Inverness.

That afternoon James received the crushing news. Immediately afterwards he was called away on a business matter which kept him from home for the rest of the day. Next afternoon he sent for a Stewart notary, the father of the Charles who had served the injunction. The old man was out fishing and his eventual reply, which consisted of a refusal to act due to exhaustion, did not reach Aucharn until early on Thursday morning. With the evictions only twenty-four hours away James penned a letter to Charles begging him to come to Aucharn that evening. He had decided that his best course was to advise the tenants to refuse to vacate their dwellings unless they were threatened with military force, and pin his hopes on the Barons' vetoing the evictions. Glenure was to be confronted by an assembly consisting of the younger Stewart lawyer, the tenants and some persons of standing. The two Ballachulishes had agreed to fill the latter roles. The son

16

was down for assizer duty on the day, but decided to risk a hefty fine by absenting himself. If the factor's papers were in order the group would protest formally at the proceedings and inform him of their refusal to obey the decree.

While these preparations were going on in Appin, Glenure's mission to Lochaber was meeting with mixed fortunes. On arrival at Maryburgh he was chagrined to learn that the sheriff-substitute of Inverness-shire was not in residence, which meant that he could not obtain the warrant to remove the Mamore tenants. Next day he sent a message to the landlord of the Kentallen Inn, who was himself set down for eviction, telling him to prepare to entertain him and some others on Thursday evening. In so doing Glenure may have pronounced his own doom, for by Wednesday half the countryside knew he would return next day. Not only that, but his route could be predicted with something close to certainty. On that morning the factor called to see Charles Stewart the notary and showed him a copy of the Court of Session document revoking James's sist. Stewart told him he had received a letter from a junior colleague of the Edinburgh solicitor who had advised James to present the Bill of Suspension. That petition, claimed the colleague, had contained falsehoods. He, Stewart, had forwarded the letter to James. Almost certainly the notary there and then told Glenure that he would no longer act for the tacksman, for at the trial he stated that he declined to serve 'because he did not care to disoblige Glenure'.

A day later Red Colin rode out to his death escorted by Mungo and Mackenzie. On his way south he visited some tenants, confirmed them in their leases for the coming year and gained their agreement to take the oath. At North Ballachulish he caught up with Donald Kennedy, whom he had sent forward on foot. Kennedy was a sheriff's officer whose duty it was to supervise the evictions. The factor's party was detained for more than an hour by a deputation of villagers protesting against his plans for the appointment of a regular boatman on the Ballachulish ferry. With the dispute unresolved Glenure and the others embarked on the short passage across the narrows to Appin. They proceeded for about half a mile along the margin of the loch, then veered left onto the path through the wood. Seven or eight minutes later, by Mungo's estimate, the assassin's shot put an end to Glenure's problems and raised those of James to new and perilous heights.

At dusk a sombre group ringed the corpse. In addition to the dead man's travelling companions there were the laird of Ballachulish and his people, Ballieveolan's sons and some Glen Duror men, including one of James's servants. The tacksman was absent: his wife had implored him not to go for fear of armed Campbells. The corpse was carried down the hillside to the loch and transported by boat to Kentallen, where it was lodged in the inn. On the following day it was examined by two surgeons, one of whom performed an autopsy. Their reports differed in details but agreed in their conclusion: Glenure was killed by two bullets which entered his back on each side of the spine and emerged a few inches apart just below the navel. As the three survivors of the ambush were sure they had heard only one shot – and their testimony on this point was to be endorsed by two other men – it was clear that the musket-balls had been fired at a single discharge. It was a common practice among hunters of the period to insert two balls, one larger than the other, in the muzzle. The proximity of the entry wounds postulated a shot from very close range. None of these judgments became a subject of dispute.

On the next evening James was at an alehouse a few hundred yards from Aucharn. There appeared a party of men which included Mungo and Ballieveolan. They were attended by a squad of soldiers whose officer arrested James and his elder son, a young man in his early or mid twenties. He was usually called Allan Beg ('Little Allan'), probably to distinguish him from an older foster-brother of the same name, but it may be helpful in this book to call him Allan Oig ('Young Allan') to avoid confusion over similar names. Also arrested was one of James's farm-hands. All walked to Aucharn, where a valedictory dram was drunk. Then the prisoners were taken to their cells in the fort.

2 The Investigation

THE INVESTIGATING FORCE was fully in its stride before the body was buried. Letters, borne as speedily as public messengers and horsemen could deliver them, criss-crossed Argyll summoning sixty law officers and relatives. The military were deployed in large numbers. Gossip had it that 200 were quartered at Appin House, the residence of Dugald, chief of the Appin Stewarts. Seven hundred persons were precognosed, a precognition being a preliminary examination to determine if there are grounds for a prosecution. The population of Appin was then estimated at 2800. Such a huge injection of manpower to track the murderer of an obscure official can be understood only in its setting. In 1752 the Highlands hummed with rumours of an imminent rising. Two years earlier the Young Pretender, obsessed with his dream of restoring the Stuart monarchy, had ordered the delivery of 26 000 muskets. With characteristic dash he slipped across the Channel from Antwerp and conferred with his supporters in London. He inspected the Tower of London's defences and remarked that a gate could be blown in by a petard. To blunt the edge of anti-Catholic hostility he was formally received into the Church of England. These aggressive moves may have been the early steps in what became known as the Elibank Plot, which took its name from its main organiser, a headstrong and violent brother of Lord Elibank. St James's Palace and the Tower were to be seized in a sudden onslaught, while a large Swedish contingent would invade Scotland. Their landing was to sound a tocsin that would bring the rebel clans marching into Crieff in columns of white cockades. A general insurrection would ensue, the date set for the *coup* being 10 November. By the spring preparations were well under way and the prince and his exiled retinue were putting the final touches to their plans. Communications between the Highlands and the plotters on the Continent were fitful, but enough information filtered through to alert the clans to the

19

momentous prospects in the air. In London the Government was even more aware of looming danger, though not of its fine details. A team of agents which included a spy in the prince's network of collaborators kept it amply briefed on the conspirators' designs. Inevitably this intelligence was passed on to the Campbells, the Administration's staunchest allies in Scotland, who were best placed to quell a sudden eruption. The powerful tribe was capable of mustering 3000 men, at a conservative guess. As its dominance had been achieved largely by the ability to analyse the political chessboard with unblinking realism it is unlikely that it needed much schooling on the plot.

Glenure's murder at a moment when the country was alive with menacing rumours shocked his clan in several different ways. At the purely human level they were filled with horror at the barbarous shooting from behind of a tolerant, unarmed man, the father of two infant daughters and husband of a pregnant girl who had barely entered her twenties. As guardians of the Hanoverian peace they were galled by what they took to be a deliberate challenge to the regime. Some may even have thought it might be the starting signal for the rising whose imminence was being whispered through the glens. On all counts it could not go unpunished.

The hunt was co-ordinated by Glenure's half-brother, John Campbell of Barcaldine, who is commemorated in local legend as Iain Du, 'Black John', from the colour of his hair. Born at the turn of the century, he was believed to be the first man to have struck a blow for King George in the 'Forty-five. A band of rebels crossed Loch Creran and kidnapped some of his people with the object of pressing them into the Stuart service. Barcaldine and his men pursued the raiders by night across the water and forced them to flee, leaving their prisoners behind. He served without pay as a captain of militia in the rebellion. A sufferer from gout – 'your old acqueintance', as one of his half-brothers jocosely referred to it – he showed much of the irascibility unfairly associated with that affliction. He was not only numbed and

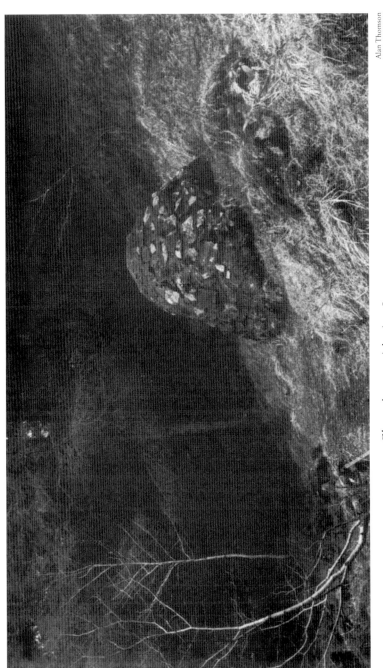

Glenure's memorial cairn, Lettermore

Lettermore wood as seen from Onich

Fort William and Maryburgh c. 1745

Sheriff Stonefield
'Like many corpulent men he was blessed with vitality. . .'

grieved by Glenure's death but consumed with indignation. His brother had been martyred while carrying out the orders of a government which suspected him of treachery. Barcaldine was a factor on three estates, and he had simmered under the same cloud of suspicion that darkened Glenure's last days. He too had been pricked out for dismissal by Pelham, a decision that cannot have failed to enrage him, as he was unrelated to the Camerons. He now embarked on the quest for the killer with a passion that often took him beyond the borders of legality.

Equally dedicated were the numerous Campbell gentry who threw their energies into the investigation. Barcaldine's son Mungo took up residence at Fort William at the commander's request. He was present at the interrogation of some of the witnesses and used his lawyer's skill in examination. The dead man's full brother Duncan, now his heir presumptive, made his headquarters at Glenure House. A lazy, clever skinflint, he was a sheriff-substitute, or a deputy chief law enforcement agent, of Perthshire. Overall responsibility for recording precognitions in Appin was in the hands of Archibald Campbell of Stonefield. A sheriff for decades, he was a stickler for the formulae of the law. Like many corpulent men he was blessed with vitality, combining his peace-keeping duties with those of successful man of business and Commissioner of Supply. Four days after the murder he had arrived in the district and taken down the first statements. He set up his command post at Inshaig, in all probability in the alehouse where James was arrested. It seems certain that the precognitions were destroyed after the trial, as was the normal practice, but copies of many of the most crucial depositions have unaccountably survived. They were discovered two centuries later by Lieutenant-General Sir William MacArthur, who embodied many of their new revelations in his book *The Appin Murder and the Trial of James Stewart*. The copies are inscribed in an unlined notebook whose title page reads: *Precognitions taken in the Base Murder of Colin Campbell of Glenure Esqr.* Its contents, one hundred and fifty declarations and four letters, are written in at least two different hands. Brackets, lettered in alphabetical sequence, are used in the margins to mark significant passages. Plainly the writings were transcribed from the originals to provide the Lord Advocate with the facts on which to build his indictment. They may also have been studied by the sheriffs, justices of the peace and other enquiry officers as an aid to their pursuit. The authenticity of the notebook has been called in question because of its lack of autograph signatures, but a close scrutiny of the material reveals the extreme unlikelihood of malpractice. Any partisan of James would have doctored many statements that were damaging to his cause, and his detractors would unquestionably have edited Mungo's precognition, for reasons that will become clear.

At his first session Stonefield interviewed a Campbell inn-keeper who swore that a recent customer of his named Allan Breck Stewart emitted sulphurous threats against the lives of Glenure and Ballieveolan 'and prayed God that he & Glenure wou'd meet by themselves before he left the Country . . .' Allan's name was already at the forefront of Stonefield's mind; it had rung around Appin as the chief suspect within a day or two of the murder. An even more startling rumour was sweeping through the area that Ardsheal himself had recently landed in Scotland and was hiding in Perthshire. When young he had enrolled himself among the heroes of his clan by crossing blades in a friendly duel with Rob Roy, and drawing blood. Though well on in years in 1745 – an English prisoner described him as 'a big fat man, troubled with lethargy' – he led the Appin Regiment, carbine in hand. He was one of the rebel leaders excluded from pardon under the terms of the Act of Indemnity, a proscription which added to his glory. His reported presence in the country so soon after the assassination must have struck the law officers as anything but coincidental, especially if they had heard the tattle that he had sent back a message from France to the effect that all his friends in Appin must be dead if Glenure was allowed to carry on as he did. A notice was rushed to the investigators ordering them 'to search for and apprehend the persons of the said Charles Stewart and of the said Allan Stewart, alias Breck . . .' No sighting of Ardsheal was thereafter recorded, and the rumour must be dismissed as just that.

Allan Breck's history marked him out as a promising candidate for the role of sharpshooter. He was born at Invercomrie, at the west end of Loch Rannoch, where his mother still lived. According to one old tale of uncertain origin his father was a 'broken man', that is, one whose acts of criminality were so outrageous that he was outlawed by the authorities or his own clan. Certainly Rannoch was at the time a favoured bolt-hole of ruffians of every variety. Allan's father died young, attended in his last illness by old Ballachulish, whom he told that he intended to leave the care of his children to Ardsheal and James. The boy went to live with James at Auchindarroch and grew up there. His nickname 'Breck' was derived from the Gaelic word for 'spotted', and referred to his heavily pock-marked face, the legacy of a childhood bout of smallpox. As a young man he speedily ran through what few possessions his father left him and accumulated debts which his adoptive parents were indulgent enough to settle. Tilling the soil held no thrill for his adventurous soul so he took the King's shilling and joined an English regiment. When Prince Charles let slip the dogs of war Allan Breck, to his probable dismay, found himself in arms against his own clansmen. At Prestonpans he was captured and promptly defected to the Highland Army. Whether he fought at Culloden is not known, but he shared the privations of Ardsheal through the long months when he lay in the heather scanning the horizon for a French sail. They eventually obtained passage across the sea. His whereabouts during the next two years is a matter of conjecture but it is likely that he spent them with Ardsheal at Sens, deer-hunting on the archbishop's lands. On 11 January 1749 he enlisted in Ogilvy's Regiment, a French army unit composed of exiled Scots. The inducting officer recorded the details, with a brief physical description of the recruit. In the summer of 1752, when a muster-roll was drawn up, the clerk gave an expanded sketch of Allan. As it has never appeared in print it is worth setting down here, in translation: 'Allan Stuart Native of Argile in Scotland aged 26 years Height 5 feet 6 inches 1 line Hair black curly face long extremely marred by smallpox scars eyes grey and deep-set nose long mouth ordinary.' It should be noted that the age mentioned is that given on the day of his enlistment, and that the French units of measurement did not correspond exactly to their English equivalents. By imperial reckoning he was just over 5 feet 10 inches. A point to be remembered is that his eyes were grey, not dark, as the sheriffs' handbills alleged. The informant who supplied that detail must have been misled by black eyebrows over sunken eyes. Allan's regimental duties were not so onerous as to prevent him from making extended trips to his homeland. His purpose, it was said, was to drum up recruits for the French army, to carry intelligence between the Jacobites in both countries, and to convey 'second rents' to exiled lairds. Interspersed with these secret activities were public appearances in the houses and grog-shops of Appin and Rannoch. An affable and popular man when sober, he turned ugly in his cups. Of his nerve there can be no question, for as a defector in time of war he risked the rope every time he set foot in Scotland. A chance encounter with an army patrol or a convivial evening in the wrong dram-house could have been the end of him.

A nationwide manhunt was now launched by the lawmen. Letters sped to customs officers at ports, enclosing a description of the soldier. To an accurate depiction of his features, excepting his eyes, they added that he was 'a little Innknee'd, Round Shoulder'd, about Thirty years of age . . .'. A newspaper report described him as 'shabby with an inclination to be genteel'. The naval sloop *Porcupine* sailed to the Firth of Forth, there to detain any suspect vessels. The king being absent in Hanover, the Lords Justices – the cabinet, that is – used their power of regency to order that a notice be pinned to every church door in Argyll offering a reward of £100 for information leading to the arrest of every participant tried and convicted. A free pardon was dangled before any plotter who effected the capture and successful prosecution of his accomplices, provided that he himself had not fired the shot. Glenure's relatives offered a bounty of the same amount. Some of them thought the Government's inducement niggardly but tactfully did not outbid it. By 23 May the meticulous Stonefield had examined sixty-one persons, from whose testimony the officers constructed a version of the supposed intrigue which they were never to abandon. It held that the murder was planned by James and Allan Breck on Monday, 11 May. On that day the defector came to Aucharn dressed in a black-feathered hat, a knee-length blue coat with yellow metal buttons, red vest, black breeches and tartan hose. The coat was part of his regimental uniform. He stayed overnight and left next morning wearing a blue bonnet, a dun greatcoat over a short black jacket, and blue trousers with white stripes. The stripes created a plaid or chequered pattern, the closest approach to the forbidden tartan that Highlanders dared wear. This outfit, the theory ran, was furnished by James as a fitter camouflage for a killer designate. Allan set off on a round of visits that took him to Ballachulish, Carnoch and Callert. At Carnoch he announced that if the incoming tenants sent in their cattle he would drive the animals away. On Wednesday evening he returned and slept at Ballachulish House. Stonefield and his men were convinced that Breck plotted this apparently haphazard route to ensure an encounter with Glenure, circling his prey like a predatory shark. At eleven or twelve o'clock on Thursday he borrowed a fishing-rod and started angling in the burn close to the house. Presently he moved upstream out of sight. Not long after midday the Ballachulish ferryman saw him near the south slip. He then made his way to the point of ambush a mile away. After shooting the factor he fled to Carnoch where in the early hours of the next morning he knocked up John, the young chief of the Macdonalds of Glencoe, and his stepmother.

She reported a tense conversation verbatim. 'What news?' she asked him.

'There is enough of news this day in the country. Glenure is shot dead.'

'God bless me!' she exclaimed. 'Where?'

'In the woods of Lettermore.'

'When?'

'Yesterday evening.'

She invited him in for a meal but he declined, bade them goodbye and moved off.

Such was the chronicle pieced together by the pursuers in a mere five days. They had achieved it in the teeth of lies and omissions by some of those who had most to lay bare. Then came a revelation that can be seen as the first crack in the dam. It was inspired by the governor of Fort William, Colonel Crawfurd, whose impatience with legal nuances matched that of Barcaldine. He had lodged John Beg Maccoll, the servant who had been arrested with James, in a cell with a condemned prisoner, 'to try what Effects the Exhortations of the Clergy would produce', as he put it. John Beg was the messenger James had sent to his lawyer on the day of the murder, a circumstance which made him in Colonel Crawfurd's eyes a possible accomplice, if not worse. The tiny farm-hand remained tight-lipped, so the governor tried another tack. He offered him a modest bribe to confess where James had hidden his weapons. Disconcerted, and lured by the money, John Beg admitted that he and Dugald Maccoll, another of his master's labourers, had concealed them in the brae after the shooting. Crawfurd despatched this information to Inshaig, where Barcaldine and a small infantry detachment were contributing their aid to Stonefield. Dugald Maccoll was fetched and re-examined. Under interrogation he turned faint and had to be revived with water. He confirmed that he and John Beg had hidden two muskets on the hill above the farmhouse, a disclosure which instantly raised the hopes of the lawmen sky-high. Later that evening Charles, James's younger son, saw a squad of soldiers advance up the hill towards the cache. He dashed out and hurried to the spot by another route. When he got there he was seized by some of Barcaldine's men who, prudently, had been sent ahead. Dugald was with the military party that located the hiding-place, from which two muskets and four broadswords were brought to light. The longer gun was loaded, the shorter not. The experienced squad captain concluded that both had been discharged not long before, but naturally fixed his attention on the smaller, unloaded musket with the larger bore. Its lock was held in place by a single screw instead of the customary two. A stick tied with string to the stock acted as a makeshift splint. To test whether the gun had recently been fired a few men, including the captain, inserted a finger in the muzzle and each time it came out black. A local smith later stated that in February James's son Allan Oig had employed him to repair the lock. This was the murder weapon, the law officers decided, and nothing in the surviving papers suggests that they afterwards wavered in their conviction. Barcaldine and the soldiers completed a triumphant evening by ransacking Aucharn and taking away a number of James's papers and a black jacket belonging to Allan Oig.

'. . . we have broke the Ice,' crowed Colonel Crawfurd in a letter to his commanding general, and he expressed no more than the truth. Some witnesses were re-questioned and changed their stories or vouchsafed knowledge they had withheld. Fresh examinees divulged new facts, fleshing out the skeletal case against James and Allan Breck. At the end of the first week in July the investigators judged that they had assembled sufficient evidence to present to a court, though they were far from confident that it would win a verdict to their liking. It is instructive to cast an eye over the story that emerged from the precognitions, as Barcaldine must have seen it.

Allan Breck's first recorded intimation of violence came on New Year's Day, 1750. He said that Glenure deserved to be shot for taking the factorship. James retorted 'that such a method was not to be taken'. This testimony, given by a Cameron who was in the company, was not used by the prosecutors at the trial, presumably because it showed James in a pacific light. Breck's next minatory utterance took place some weeks before the murder, when he told Dugald Maccoll that the people of Appin were lifeless for not putting a stop to Glenure's career. Shortly thereafter he took off on a drinking binge with a crony. While in a group that included a Campbell alehouse-keeper he reviled Glenure and Ballicvcolan for their greed and injustice in turning out the residents. 'I would rather the devil in hell have the factory (factorship) than Glenure,' he stormed. Later that night, in the Campbell's own tavern, Allan told him to tell his two friends that if they continued to oppress the tenants he would make blackcocks of them – current slang for shoot them. He said that the factor had told Colonel Crawfurd that he, Allan Breck, had come from France as Ardsheal's spy. He repeated several times his threat to get even with Red Colin before he left the country. On another night of the spree a poor man entered the alehouse. Allan asked his friend to deliver two pecks of meal to the pauper. When the man thanked him he told him, 'If you will bring to me the skin of the Red Fox I will give you what is better than the meal I ordered for you.' This striking turn of speech caught the fancy of Robert Louis Stevenson when his father presented him with the book of the trial. In his *Kidnapped* and *Catriona*, the core of whose plots is the murder in Lettermore, Glenure is transfigured and immortalised as the Red Fox. Only Allan Breck is known to have applied the sobriquet to the real man, and that on this single occasion.

As has been mentioned, James's earliest threat – his confession that he would like to take a shot at Glenure – was breathed in the period when he was being removed from Auchindarroch. The factor was not the only target of his abuse. He told a herdsman who entered the service of the usurper Ballieveolan that 'it should be Remembered to him as long as he lived and that if he did not meet with Resentment himself his friends

28

would meet with it after his Death.' A year later, while Breck was fulminating in the Appin drinking-dens, James, on his ride to Edinburgh to seek the injunction, was likewise sounding off in bellicose terms. After breakfasting at an inn he called for a dram. His table companion, a merchant named Colin Maclaren, suggested that he should help the landlord to part of it. In his precognition the Campbell landlord swore '. . . James answered he did not know in what manner he wou'd help him the Deponent or any of his name, unless it were to the gallows.' The innkeeper expressed wonder that his guest should hold an entire clan to blame for the acts of one of its members. James insisted that if Glenure had treated the landlord as he had treated him he would have disliked him to the same degree. The tacksman resumed his journey south with Maclaren. They stopped at another alehouse, where James launched afresh on his tirade against the object of his fury. He claimed that he had challenged Glenure to fight with pistols and he refused. The travellers rode off again, pausing to drop in at a third dram-house. Maclaren's precognition has not come down to us, but if we cautiously assume that its contents did not differ radically from the evidence he gave at the trial we learn of James's most pertinent hint of assassination. When they rode out again the little blusterer, by now far gone in drink, carried on condemning the evictions despite his partner's efforts to change the subject. If he should fail in Edinburgh, James pronounced, he would take his case to Parliament, and if he was unsuccessful there – and here he paused before stating with emphasis – he would have to take the sole remedy that remained.

On the fatal day, it will be remembered, James sent a letter to Charles Stewart the notary in Maryburgh. The courier was John Beg, whose precognition is also no longer extant. Fortunately it is extremely unlikely that its absence affects our knowledge of any essential detail of the case. As well as delivering the letter John Beg's instructions were to collect some money from William the merchant, who was James's cousin and brother-in-law, for cattle the tacksman had bought on his behalf. William told John Beg that he had sent his master a letter that morning about the cattle, and the servant went off empty-handed. He made such speed on the way back that he arrived at Aucharn before William's messenger.

In the wake of the tragedy next morning James appealed again to William. His emissary this time was Alexander Stewart, known to all as Sandy Bane ('Fair-haired Sandy'), a family friend. A pedlar and first cousin of Allan Breck, he was briefed to ask for five English pounds or guineas as an advance on the cost of the cows. The cash, James explained, was to finance Breck's departure from the country. Sandy Bane walked to Maryburgh and made the plea. William said he was out of funds but his wife told the messenger to come back on the morrow and he would get the money. Sandy Bane went to Glen Nevis, where he had agreed to carry out another errand for James, and returned next day. William's wife met him in the street and gave him three guineas. When the pedlar reached Aucharn in the evening James had just been arrested. The squad officer permitted his prisoner a private word with his wife Margaret and Sandy. From his purse the tacksman took two guineas and gave them to Margaret, instructing her to send them, together with the three borrowed at Maryburgh, to Allan Breck. He asked Sandy Bane to act as bearer and to take the soldier's showy clothes with him. After supper, when James had been escorted towards the fort, Margaret gave the pedlar the money and clothing. She asked him to take them to a grazing-farm at Caolasnacon managed by a man named John Don or Breck Maccoll. There he would find the fugitive. Under cover of darkness Sandy left Aucharn and set off on the ten-mile hike, fetching up at his destination early on Sunday morning. Cautiously he hid the garments at the root of a tree before approaching John Don's house. He met the man outside. John Don, like Sandy, was to play a decisive part in the affair. Aged forty, he was employed as a stockman by the laird of Appin. His duty was to rear his master's beasts, and he reaped a share of the profits from their sale. The post was a responsible one for which James had recommended him to Appin. He now denied that he had seen Allan Breck, but on learning that Sandy had brought supplies for him he admitted that the soldier had already established contact.

The meeting had taken place on the preceding afternoon. While cutting firewood John Don heard a whistle. He looked up and saw Allan in the heugh of Corrynakiegh, a deep, leafy fissure etched by a lusty stream that runs down the Pap of Glencoe. He was wearing a dun greatcoat over a black jacket and trousers of blue plaid. The stockman told his visitor that he would certainly be suspected of the murder; rumour was rife that Allan was one of two men seen fleeing the site. Allan protested his innocence, adding that he had heard that there was only one killer. James and his son Allan Oig were sure to be arrested, he went on, but there could be no proof against them 'unless their own Tongues betrayed them . . .'. He asked John Don to fetch him money from Aucharn and meal from Lady Glencoe, but he refused. Allan then fashioned a quill pen from a wood-pigeon's feather he picked up under the trees. He wrote a letter appealing for cash and asked the stockman to take it to William the merchant. This request too was turned down. Allan said he was surprised that no money had arrived for him 'though it was promised . . .'. He then returned to his secure refuge among the birch bushes of Corrynakiegh to await the advent of the currency.

No doubt John Don recounted much of this interview to Sandy Bane when he showed up next morning. The pedlar in turn reported the arrest of James and Allan Oig, and that Allan Breck's name was on every lip. He handed over the five guineas, pointed out the spot where he had hidden the French attire, bedded down for a nap, then set out for Glen Duror. That night Allan Breck knocked at the stockman's window. John Don went out and gave him the clothes and cash. He broke the news that James and his son were prisoners at the fort. Allan said he was more worried about Allan Oig than his father, as he feared that the younger man was less able to keep his secrets.

He asked John Don to meet him early next morning to collect James's clothing and restore them to their owner or Margaret. Before sunrise the grazier went to the meeting-place, to find no one there. Allan Breck had left his foster-father's garb to be picked up. One of the jacket pockets contained a powder-horn of a flat design. Red wax had been used to seal a crack on the inside. Two months later John Don guided a military detail to a cleft in a rock where he had hidden the items.

By the middle of July the case against James and the fugitive consisted of the foregoing summary of facts extracted from the precognitions. It made a fairly convincing if sketchy narrative, but two of its key witnesses were of questionable value. By a coincidence which no fictionist would dare invent, Colin Maclaren, James's travelling companion, was a friendly acquaintance, if not an outright crony, of Glenure's younger brother Robert. The two men had been fellow apprentices of a Stirling merchant and both had taken up business careers in that town. The closeness of their relationship is illustrated by the fact that a few days after the murder Robert wrote from Appin to his former master, adding that in the event of his being absent the letter was to be passed to Maclaren. This firm personal tie obviously called in question Maclaren's objectivity as a witness, and a well-briefed defence counsel could exploit it to the full. John Don too looked an unreliable foundation on which to build a case. His disclosures, indispensable in the framing of an indictment, contained several dubious elements. In his first examination on 4 June he never referred to his meetings with Allan Breck and Sandy. A month later, when re-questioned, he allowed that he had lied to Sandy about not having seen the soldier. He said that Breck had arranged a final meeting to effect the hand-over of James's clothes but did not divulge that the transfer had taken place or that he had hidden the clothes. At his third interrogation he told the story set out above and did not thenceforth depart from it. But however much the lawmen may have doubted the details of his version they cannot have failed to be elated by the revelation that

James sent escape money to the chief suspect. More significant than the act of giving aid was that he knew where to send it. The fact that it was Margaret who directed Sandy to Caolasnacon did not deflect the investigators from their conviction that she had got her information from her husband. And they must have perceived with satisfaction that not a word of evidence had surfaced to show that the tacksman had learned of Allan Breck's hideout *after* the two men parted on 11 May. These circumstances, when added to the threats, Allan's donning of James's clothes and the discovery of the gun, contributed to assuring the Campbells that they were on the right track.

The conscientious Stonefield did not neglect other suspects, and high on his list was James's son, Allan Oig. At Aucharn the sheriff uncovered a copy of a letter signed with the young man's name and addressed to a cousin. It was dated 1 April 1751, a month or so after Allan's family had been removed from Auchindarroch to make way for Ballieveolan. The writer complained that Glenure planned to take the Ardsheal estate into his exclusive management, and that Ballieveolan was actively manoeuvring to occupy Glen Duror. '. . . however it shall be a Dear Glen to them or (ere) they shall have it.' This was taken to hold a hint of violence, but Allan Oig's defenders were to explain that he meant merely that it would cost them plenty. Allan denied that he had written it.

Since it is abundantly evident that the law officers suspected that he might have shot the factor or restored the gun to Aucharn, or both, Allan Oig's alibi for the murder day must be studied as keenly as the scanty facts permit. By his own account he went out for a morning walk up the glen. While strolling back he told two women to keep their cattle off his father's land. He saw a man passing, who, one of the women said, had been enquiring about Glenure. The stranger was then walking towards Auchindarroch, that is, on a course that would take him in the direction of the wood. Allan Oig returned to Aucharn. His brother Charles said that the suspect then accompanied him, their sister and a girl visitor to Inshaig, a tiny settlement no more than five minutes' walk from their home. It is overwhelmingly probable that the four young people spent the afternoon and early evening at the dram-house where James was arrested. There cannot have been more than a very few houses at Inshaig; of the 139 persons who gave recorded testimony in precognitions or the trial the pub landlord alone hailed from the remote spot. Allan Oig's alibi was supported by one of the farm labourers who affirmed that the young master was at home from midday onwards but had gone off, he had been told, to Inshaig. According to Charles, Allan left Inshaig and walked the brief distance home shortly before John Beg came to Inshaig and announced Glenure's death. This evidence, if true, places Allan Oig in his native glen until well after the factor died. But how watertight is it? Of other direct testimony we have only the statements of Allan himself, but there are compelling reasons for believing that his alibi stands up. When questioned, Charles alone of the rest of his family was interrogated about Allan Oig's movements, to judge from their replies. Preliminary questioning must have elicited that the suspect was indeed in Glen Duror when the shot rang out. No statement by the girl visitor has lasted, nor have those of the other witnesses with whom the sheriffs must have checked these stories. If they failed to support Allan's alibi we may be sure that their precognitions would have been included among those that have endured. The objection that these were members of his family and friends who could be expected to lie loyally to save him can be countered by the declaration of one of his shooting companions. He said he saw Allan Oig a day or two after the tragedy and that he 'shewed no Concern for the murder altho it was the subject of Conversation.' He reported a talk he had had with the girl visitor at about the same time, when she told him that James was as cheerful as usual and showed no signs of regret at Glenure's demise. Katharine, James's dairymaid, who was present when Mackenzie blurted the news, told Stonefield that her master spoke no word of condolence on hearing it.

Clearly there were some Appin folk who were affronted by what they took to be their callousness. That they would have subscribed to a false story for Allan Oig is very difficult to believe. It is just as incredible that the sheriffs would have been unable to break a fraudulent alibi that relied on four known witnesses and possibly a few unknown ones at Inshaig. There is evidence in a page entitled *Memorial anent Glenure's Murder* that the hunters gave up trying to establish that the young man was present at the site of the ambush. The unsigned and unaddressed piece makes the point that James made sure that all his family were well away from the scene. By this nimble volte-face the lawmen seem to have persuaded themselves that Allan Oig's absence from Lettermore was more incriminating than his attendance would have been. Hence all the indications are that a quick conclusion was reached that he did not go to the wood that day but was sufficiently concerned in the plot to warrant continued imprisonment until further discoveries should unveil his role. They gave out that he had been jailed to prevent him from tampering with witnesses.

Another promising suspect was Red Ewan Maccoll, a brother of John Don. He was a former tenant of Ardsheal and a frequent caller at Aucharn. Among those who died in the Appin Regiment at Culloden were eighteen Maccolls, some of whom may well have fallen to Campbell bullets, so there was no need to speculate too widely on a possible motive for Red Ewan. It emerged that he spent a lot of time at Aucharn in the week of the murder, and twice offered the opinion – if Allan Oig's word can be believed – 'that it was hard in Glenure to turn out the honest Tennants of the Ardshiel Estate . . .'. He had made up his mind to join the party that would protest to the factor on the term day. When set beside the information that John Don owned a gun and that at the time of the murder Red Ewan was the possessor of a dun jacket and dun breeches, the case against him took on a menacing aspect. It will be recalled that Mungo Campbell described the fleeing gunman as wearing such a garb. To judge from the precognitions, the questioners swiftly decided he was not dressed in those clothes on the relevant day, for two witnesses are briefly recorded as saying that he wore a short coat. Further succour arrived for the suspect in the form of an alibi. In the late afternoon of the murder day a number of men were drinking in an alehouse at Tigh-phuirt, a hamlet four miles from Lettermore. One of them, James Stewart, eldest son of the laird of Fasnacloich, deposed that Red Ewan joined the company between six and seven o'clock. A cousin of Fasnacloich's who was in the party implied that the man had got there slightly earlier. From his statement, which was ambiguous, one could take the meaning that Red Ewan had been present for some time when Glencoe took out his watch and said that the hour was between six and seven. This alehouse evidence was fortified by the testimony of John Don, his servant-girl and a neighbour that the stockman's gun was still at Caolasnacon when Red Ewan set off for Tigh-phuirt. The investigators decided that he was blameless, evidently in the belief that he could not have covered the ground between Lettermore and the tavern in about an hour. Although the distance between them was not great the intervening terrain would have made the feat a near impossibility. A straight flight through the wood and along the high road could not have gone unobserved in a comparatively highly populated area, and a devious route skirting the ferry and other peopled centres would have been extremely difficult in the time. Some students of the case have judged the lawmen to be naive. Couldn't Red Ewan have slipped out unnoticed from a crowded and carefree drinking-room, they ask, done the deed and covertly returned? Or did they wilfully ignore the evidence against him, letting him off the hook in the hope of landing a bigger fish?

Another man who attracted instant suspicion was young Fasnacloich, who is believed to have captained his local company of the Appin Regiment and led and bled at Culloden. Now an unreformed dissenter, his ferocious language and shadowy movements had once or twice caught the attention of the authorities. When Ballieveolan took over the tacksman's farm Fasnacloich told a Campbell that if he had been a friend or near relation of Ardsheal he would have shot the supplanter through the head. He later flayed another Campbell who had obtained a lease on Ardsheal land in these words: 'You are greedy people who will not be contented with your own lands but will remove other poor people from their possessions.' His antagonist retorted that his clan would be in the middle of Appin in spite of him, to which Fasnacloich replied that if he were a close relative of Ardsheal he would be the death of them before they got a foothold there. He and Allan Oig, with two other men, had formed a shooting party on the island of Balnagowan, a retreat favoured by hunters because of its remoteness, a fortnight before Glenure's death. Fasnacloich and one of the others were caught and fined. Allan Breck spent the weekend before the murder at his home, and two days later they met at Ballachulish House and walked together to Carnoch. Breck left for Callert and young Fasnacloich did not see him again. It seemed to Barcaldine's son Alexander, who was certain that Breck had fired the shot, that he could not have spent so much time in his friend's company without disclosing his lethal purpose. Local gossip reported that Fasnacloich had not been seen in the district since the killing and that he was in Perthshire visiting friends. A warrant was issued for his arrest and the lawmen set afoot enquiries as to whether he, his cousin or Glencoe carried guns that day. On his return he was precognosed, but divulged nothing incriminating against himself or Allan Breck. At his second examination he told of his presence in the alehouse at the vital time, thereby exculpating both himself and Red Ewan. Young Fasnacloich remained at liberty, but the peace officers were far from satisfied that he had not played an active part in the course of events. A month later, when the conviction had taken root that the assassination was the result of a fair-sized conspiracy, they considered jailing him. Mungo urged that he should be confined at Inveraray, doubtless in the hope that a stretch in the citadel of Campbell power might make him more talkative. The proposal was never put into effect.

37

Other possible snipers were scrutinised. James's labourers Dugald and John More were quickly cleared when it was learned that they spent the day carting casks of ale from Kentallen to their master's house. Young Callert came into the reckoning on the strength of the rumour that he was recruiting killers to do away with Glenure. Callert visited Aucharn on the Sunday night before the murder and may have slept there. As his precognition has not survived we must assume that he satisfied his interrogators. Young Ballachulish was one of those vetted for possession of a gun. James was known as his tutor, a flexible term which in this case seems to have meant a semi-avuncular, unofficial mentor. Ballachulish had a conversation with Breck at the former's home two days before the murder, and on the next night he went to Aucharn and discussed the evictions with James. They agreed that resistance was the right course. He travelled to Appin House on the following, and crucial, day and spent it with his chief. This obviously ruled him out as the slayer, but not as a conspirator.

Apart from Allan Breck the only man positively named as the murderer was Serjeant More Cameron, a Rising veteran who later raised a band of robbers, earning himself a reputation as the Robin Hood of the Highlands. He was now thought to be in France serving with one of the Scots regiments. One testifier let it be known that it was being noised around Mamore that the serjeant pulled the trigger and that Breck was beside him. James ventured the information that his foster-son told him that before leaving France the Cameron had sworn to kill Glenure for his treatment of the Mamore tenants.

Although the lawmen continued to keep all the above-mentioned suspects in their sights, as it were, nothing linking them with the murder came to view. Barcaldine and his men were reasonably confident from the start that they knew the perpetrators. This conviction was bolstered when James was questioned shortly after his arrest. He made the astonishing assertion that he had not slept at home on the Monday preceding the crime, when Breck stayed there. Writing on 24

May, Barcaldine told Colonel Crawfurd with satisfaction that he had nailed the lie. That James had slept at Aucharn was now confirmed by the whole family, he wrote, adding with bucolic innuendo 'and particularly his Wife who might have Substantial proofs of it'. James made three judicial declarations, a judicial declaration being a signed statement, not made under oath, that could be presented in evidence to a court. In his first he admitted that he had gone home that evening, but that he was so drunk he could not remember whether he had supped with Breck. The rest of his long narrative offered nothing to a prosecutor in the way of guilty revelations, but its omissions deepened the belief that here was the brains behind the plot. He said nothing of sending twice for the money or of despatching it to the soldier. The fact that he could have given a natural explanation for both actions can only have underlined their sinister possibilities. His wife and children made a total of twelve statements, nine of which were judicial declarations whose admissibility as evidence was to be hotly contested at the trial. Allan Oig's story contained no damaging material, but those of the rest of the family were to have important and unfortunate consequences for James. At their first examinations Margaret, Charles and his sister Elizabeth all said that Breck left their home on Tuesday, 12 May, in his garish French clothes. Stonefield had already learned from five witnesses that he was clad in James's jacket and trousers, and Allan Oig's dun greatcoat. Margaret also said that her husband had not owned a black jacket for nine months, a lie exposed by the very man it was invented to shield when James averred that he had lent it to Breck in April. In his fourth statement Charles in effect admitted the fictions by conceding that he had seen the French uniform at Aucharn on the day after Allan Breck left.

The decision was taken to charge James and the fugitive as accessory and principal. The investigators were under no delusion that the evidence they had amassed, while sufficient to impress the man in the tavern ingle, would meet the more rigorous demands of a courtroom. The best card in their hand

– that the tacksman knew where to send the cash – did not quite win the trick. Much of the rest of the testimony was hearsay, and therefore of doubtful legality. Undiscouraged, the zealous Barcáldine and his lieutenants renewed their efforts to underpin their case, with some success.

3 Early Reactions

ON THE DAY after his arrest and incarceration James ordered and received four bottles of spirits from cousin William. Two were for his own consumption, the others for Allan Oig, who was locked in a separate cell. Jailers of the period commonly made such a concession, with mixed motives. There are few clues to the father's state of mind during his imprisonment, but something may be gleaned from a letter he wrote on 19 May to his Edinburgh solicitor asserting that Allan Breck was generally believed to be the murderer. This process of notifying the authorities of a crime and its possible performer was colloquially called 'papering'. He described Breck and stated that he had been seen near the site of the shooting wearing his French apparel, which he also described. Though it was not claimed that he, James, or his son fired the shot, he wrote, they were suspected of foreknowledge. He was worried that his affairs would suffer at the busiest season of the year if he or Allan Oig were not released. The letter ended with an exhortation to the solicitor to bring this about, adding that Dugald Stewart of Appin and Donald Campbell of Airds would go bail for him, whatever the sum. Airds was a landowner who had rented Aucharn to James when he was forced to leave his former home. The letter, unless its author was feigning artlessness, breathes no hint that James believed himself to be in jeopardy. As a man of business he must have known enough law to be aware that the accessory to a crime was equally culpable. When that crime was murder he should have taken it for granted, if he did not already know, that bail was out of the question.

Within a week of James's imprisonment John Don joined him in the fort. At his first examination he was quizzed about his brother, Red Ewan, and his replies went a good way towards clearing him. It was only after Sandy Bane confessed their meeting at Caolasnacon that the stockman, when re-questioned, filled out his story, omitting only that he had recovered James's clothing and concealed it. On being released he met old Ballachulish two days later. The laird asked him what he had told the inquisitors. He replied that he had made several admissions which he could not withhold without perjuring himself, and that in any case his questioners knew beforehand all that he had told them. 'Poor man, I pity you,' cried the laird, by John Don's own story, 'for these people by pretending to know facts have outwitted you by drawing a confession from you.' A few days later the stockman made his last precognition. He corrected his assertion that Allan Breck knocked at his window on the Monday night; the meeting took place on Sunday. And he owned that he had collected the garments and hidden them. As the news of what was seen as John Don's defection ran through Appin he encountered undisguised hostility, and some of his friends told him the Stewarts intended to shoot him. The Ballachulishes offered him a bribe to hold fast to the interests of their clan, if his own report is to be credited. His terror reached a pitch where he imagined he saw Allan Breck three times in a week, returned to silence him for good. Convinced that the safest refuge for him was a prison cell, John Don asked the lawmen to jail him. To disguise the voluntary nature of his captivity he begged to be escorted to the fort by a military party or by Stewart of Invernahyle. They agreed to his being taken in by Invernahyle, and a cell door clanged like music behind a shackled but grateful prisoner.

After the discovery of the guns James's son Charles and the labourer Dugald swelled the ranks of detainees. A herdsman on the Ballachulish estate was probably the next to be arrested. He it was who lent Breck a fishing-rod on the morning of the tragedy. Sandy Bane was quickly pulled in, almost certainly before the end of May. A man named Carmichael was imprisoned at an undetermined date. With the exception of Ballachulish's herdsman all the above-mentioned men were still behind bars in the middle of August, and probably only he and Carmichael were released before the trial, which took place six weeks later. They were not the only persons to be apprehended. Red Ewan spent a short stay at the fort before confirmation of his presence at the Tigh-phuirt alehouse demoted him from the first rank of suspects. Breck's drinking partner, who unfortunately for himself visited Aucharn on the evening of the murder, was taken in for a while. The investigators arrested a miller named Cumming, apparently for boasting that he had inside information about the affair. The frightened fellow poured out the story of Sandy's errand for the money and its delivery to John Don. Next day the pedlar, who had said nothing of those events in an earlier statement, confessed what he knew. Cumming's name figures in the list of prosecution witnesses but he did not enter the witness-box. In all likelihood he was freed after making his important contribution. James's servants John More and Katharine the dairymaid, both surnamed Maccoll, were lodged in the tolbooth at Inveraray shortly before the trial. Katharine, a girl of sixteen, had fallen foul of Stonefield for swearing that Allan Breck had not left his clothes at Aucharn 'to her knowledge'.

Glenure's burial was delayed until 26 May to enable his widow's ailing father to recover sufficiently to attend. The cortège wended its way down Glen Creran, along the margin of the loch, then through Glen Salach to Ardchattan Priory, the ancient burial place of the Barcaldine Campbells. Red Colin's body is believed to have been laid to rest in his father's grave. No inscription records his interment – a precaution, according to a neighbourhood tradition, against desecration by the Stewarts. A year later the sheriff of Inverness, who had met the funeral expenses, was still writing to the family asking to be reimbursed.

In mid June Mungo was appointed to the factorship. He had applied for it within a week of his uncle's death, backed by Colonel Crawfurd and other weighty sponsors. On 13 June he indited an agreement reached by a family conclave which met to set the deceased's affairs in order. Sheriff Duncan took up residence in Glenure House, empowered to manage his brother's estate until the birth of the posthumous child. If the baby proved to be a boy he would inherit Glenure's possessions, as the law required. Should the child be a girl, Duncan would continue in occupation as the new laird. The dead man's quartet of premarital daughters were each left one hundred pounds. The widow, Janet, was to travel north to her father's country with her daughters to await the birth.

A week after the murder the *Edinburgh Evening Courant* told its readers that the culprits were 'some Assassins, who fired at him out of a bush . . .'. The same newspaper reproduced a letter from an unidentified brother of the slain factor, naming 'some of the Stewarts' as the killers. The journal publicised the hundred pound rewards offered by the Crown and the relatives, and printed a report that twelve persons had been confined in Fort William on suspicion of having played a part in the murder. *The Caledonian Mercury* ran a story about a man who was arrested on a ship at Leith by the crew of the *Porcupine*. He turned out to be a valet, but not before being hauled before the Lord Advocate and Lord Justice-Clerk. *The Scots Magazine* reported the assassination fairly accurately in its review of the events of May, but said that Glenure was about to eject *all* the Ardsheal tenants, 'some of whom were his near relations and all of whom had been in the late rebellion'. The periodical stated that more than one man fled the scene of the ambush.

The investigation presented the Appin Stewarts' lairds with a dilemma. If they co-operated too enthusiastically with the officials they risked the contempt of their folk, and if they withheld their assistance they courted reprisals from powerfully placed Campbells. Their chief, Dugald, was in a particularly delicate position. In spite of being created Baron Appin in the Jacobite Peerage in 1743 he had failed to lead his sept behind Prince Charles two years later. Some annalists have excused his inertia on the grounds that he was a minor, but contemporary records go a long way towards quashing that claim. Almost certainly his motive in remaining an armchair rebel was to preserve his demesnes from forfeiture. There is slender but believable evidence to suggest that by 1752 he had begun a long process of selling off his land, some of it to Campbells. In the matter of the Glenure enquiry he now steered a middle course. He tacitly endorsed the arrest of James by joining the knot of gentlemen who witnessed it, and attended the lawmen's conferences at Glenure House, but he does not seem to have used what remained of his prestige to persuade his clansmen to contribute information. He acted as a witness at several precognitions. Glenure's kinsmen distrusted him and no doubt treated him as they did his brother-in-law Invernahyle, as a potential source of disclosures but not one to confide in. Appin maintained his ambivalent stance right up to the trial, being listed as a witness for the prosecution and defence. He did not turn up, pleading his daughter's illness. The enquiry agents had instantly ruled out the possibility that Appin fired the shot, but in modern times one or two writers have wondered if they were too hasty in making up their minds. All the lies told by James's people, they argue, must have been designed to protect the one person in a clan who had to be sheltered at all costs – the chief. Unfortunately their theory does not stand up to the most cursory examination. That Appin pulled the trigger defies credence. He would have had to travel from his home to Lettermore and back, a distance of eighteen miles, through territory where his face was known to all. Of the many people who were certain to have recognised him some would have informed Stonefield when it became clear that James was in deadly danger. From all that we can learn of the younger Ballachulish, who spent the murder day at Appin House, he would never have backed his chief's alibi while his friend's life hung in the balance. No morsel of evidence exists to indicate that Appin masterminded the plot or took any part in carrying it through.

Invernahyle trod the same tightrope as Dugald. A courageous braggart, he is said to have served as second-in-command of the Appin Regiment. He visibly busied himself in the enquiry, exhibiting his keenness by inspecting the scene of the crime, but came up with no new facts. Young Barcaldine saw him as 'a poor whitty whatty body', an impression Invernahyle may have been happy to convey. Fasnacloich and Achnacone took no part in the search, the latter's name not once occurring in the documents that have defied the years. Only the Ballachulish family openly demonstrated that their prime concern was the welfare of James. On his behalf the laird consulted the ladies Callert and Glencoe, who were the prisoner's half-sisters and full siblings of Ardsheal. Ballachulish's son, who was to be revered in folk tales as Iain Buidhe, ('Yellow-haired John'), toured his relatives raising money and laying plans for the legal battles ahead. His activities did not escape the attention of young Barcaldine, who pressed his father to arrest him. The Stewart should be picked up on his way home, he suggested, when he might be carrying papers revealing the enemy intentions. It is not known how this proposal was regarded or whether any attempt was made to put it into practice, but young Ballachulish stayed at large.

A few days after the murder one of Pelham's spies in Scotland, who had possibly been sent there with a brief to probe the loyalty of the brothers Barcaldine and Glenure, reported that the victim's firm line with the disaffected was undoubtedly the cause of his death. On 24 May the Earl of Breadalbane, the head of the Campbell line of which Glenure's family was an offshoot, loosed his indignation on the Lord Chancellor, Hardwicke. Breadalbane had been a long-serving MP and ambassador to the court of St Petersburg, and his daughter Jemima was married to the Chancellor's son. He had recommended Glenure for the factorship, and his influence in high circles must have carried much weight in securing the post. In the course of the squabble over McLauchlan's farm he had sent a stiff letter to Pelham stoutly protesting his kinsman's trustworthiness. He now let the Chancellor know in pointed terms that Glenure had been killed for doing his duty despite a warning of an impending attempt on his life. He and his brother were the only factors who strictly enforced the articles of their commissions. Barcaldine had had one brother killed in the Rising and another now murdered by the rebels. This was not wholly true: the brother in the Rising had been shot in the jaw and hand, but recovered. Breadalbane may have genuinely confused his recollections or he may not, for he had a creative way with facts. The Lord Chancellor discussed the affair with the Duke of Cumberland. His Royal Highness, now execrated as 'the Butcher' for his treatment of the broken Highland Army, said that he had met both factors and trusted neither. He gave his opinion that it was Glenure's awareness that he was under suspicion that drove him to the aggressive actions which led to his destruction. Pelham wrote to the Duke of Newcastle, who was attending the king on a visit to Hanover. He asked his brother to tell His Majesty that Barcaldine's good faith could no longer be denied and that he ought to be confirmed in his post. The king willingly agreed and Pelham directed the Barons to cancel the dismissal order.

From the first, the great officials in Edinburgh and London regarded the murder as something more than the lynching of a minor functionary by rustic malcontents. Extracts from contemporary letters throw a clear light on their response.

18 May 1752: Lord Justice-Clerk Tinwald to Secretary of State Holdernesse
'I thought it greatly for his Majesty's Service, that a vigorous and thorough enquiry should be made, that, if possible the barbarous wretches, actors and accomplices in this Assassination may be discovered, & Exemplarily punisht. I have done and shall Continue to do all in my power for this purpose.'
. . . 'As soon as any Circumstances, resulting from the enquiry, come to my knowledge, I shall have the honor to lay them before your Lordship, for such a daring and execrable insult upon Government, demands the strongest attention.'

26 May 1752: Holdernesse to Tinwald
'Their Excellencies (the Lords Justices) are so highly offended,

at the Insolence of the Attempt, and the several aggravating circumstances Which attend it, That their Excellencies have determined, to offer a Reward of one Hundred Pounds, Each, to such Person or Persons, as shall discover the author, or Authors of this wicked Action . . .' . . . 'You seem so fully sensible of the dangerous Consequence of Suffering such a notorious Attack upon Government to remain unpunished, that I dare say, it is unnecessary for me, to recommend it to you, to use your utmost Diligence, for bringing the offenders to condign punishment.'

27 May 1752: Treasury Minute
'Write a Letter to the Barons in Commendation of the Endeavours to discover and bring to condign punishmt. the Actors and Accomplices in this Murder and to request them to continue their Enquiry . . .'

28 May 1752: Holdernesse to Newcastle
'There never was a more daring attempt against a Government than the murder committed in Scotland, of which I send your Grace an account by this messenger. I hope His Majesty will approve the steps that have been taken upon it. Your Grace may depend that no care or diligence shall be wanting on my part to bring the offenders to justice.'

29 May 1752: Lord Chancellor Hardwicke to Newcastle
'The King will now see that the latter, who was the younger Brother, & the most objected to, was so obnoxious to the Jacobites, & had drawn so strong a Resentment against him from that Quarter, by the faithful & zealous discharge of his Duty, that they have assassinated him.' . . . 'The Talk, or perhaps rather the Conjecture, of the Town is that the Fact was committed by one Cameron, a Bastard of the Lochiel Family, the chief of the Tenants, whom Glenuire had procured to be turned out.'

29 May 1752: Pelham to Newcastle
'And yet I cannot pass over the barbarous and audacious murder in Scotland without taking some notice of it: I hope you think we have done right here, I really think they are doing, and mean to do right in Scotland . . .' . . . 'I find a Natural brother to Stewart of Ardshiel, who is attainted, is suspected the person who committed the fact, a bold, intrepid, and as I am told, very cunning fellow.'

9 July 1752: Holdernesse to Tinwald
'I have transmitted to Hanover the Accounts you have sent up at different Times of the Steps you have taken, for the Discovery of the persons concerned in the horrid Murder of the late Mr Campbell of Glenure; and I have His Majy's Commands, to Signify to You his Royall approbation of your diligence herein, & am at the same time to recommend it to your Lordship's most serious attention, to continue to use your utmost Endeavours for bringing to Justice such barbarous Criminals.'

Bitter charges and counterblasts were to be exchanged over James's arrest and detention. A year after the trial a corrosive booklet appeared under the title *Supplement to the Trial of James Stewart by A By-Stander*. Shot through with indignation, laced with sarcasm, it was nothing less than a bare-toothed assault on the prosecutors. The anonymous scribe was widely believed to be the solicitor who acted for James at the trial – a surmise soundly based in textual clues. The booklet provoked retaliatory broadsheets angrily refuting the allegations. Among the *Breadalbane Letters* preserved in the Scottish Record Office is what appears to be a lengthy draft of an apologia for the prosecution. Since it will be necessary to refer to it from time to time in the following pages it may be useful to call it the *Justification*. Although too partisan to be believed uncritically, both these documents are valuable sources of information which would otherwise have been lost. They are at their most trustworthy when dealing with matters of public knowledge, where false statements could be immediately exposed. *By-stander* denounced James's arrest as a breach of an 'Act for preventing wrongous Imprisonment and against undue delayes in Tryals'. It laid down that the arresting official must serve the suspect with a warrant that specified the charge and was signed by the informant. He must also give him an exact copy of the warrant before locking him up. Neither of those conditions was fulfilled. The *Justification* retorted that although its author knew nothing of the circumstances of James's arrest Campbell of Airds was present and would have intervened in his capacity as justice of the peace if there had been anything irregular in the proceedings. Barcaldine had heard of his brother's death on the morning of Saturday, 16 May. He instantly wrote to the Lord Justice-Clerk in Edinburgh requesting a warrant for the arrest of James, Allan Breck and some others. Four days later the warrant, dated 17 May, was delivered to him, and he at once passed it on to Crawfurd at the fort. If he had waited for its arrival before jailing the suspect James would have fled to join Breck, whose health was now being toasted among people who should shrink from showing their faces in public lest the vengeance of Almighty God fall on them.

Shorn of its self-exonerating quibbles, this is an admission that the arrest was illegal. The tacksman's supporters were to take the view that it was only the first of a series of shifts devised to deny him his civil rights. Their version is worth relating in some detail. By 25 May the peace officers had broken the law a second time. The Act of 1701 decreed that no prisoner be kept in solitary confinement for more than eight days. James was to be held in that condition for more than a month. Even Margaret and cousin William were turned away. In the eyes of his friends his continuing isolation took on a distinctly baleful appearance. The law permitted any prisoner to apply in writing to any judge competent to try his case to fix a date for his trial. Within twenty-four hours the judge was obliged to write to the prosecutors ordering them to bring on the trial within sixty days. If they failed to do so the prisoner must be set at liberty without delay. He could be rearrested immediately on the same charge, and if the prosecutor did not try him before forty days had elapsed he had to be freed, immune from further legal action. This process was known in the vernacular as 'running the letters'. If James had gained access to a lawyer, or even a well-informed layman, he could have put the procedure in motion. In order to do so it was necessary that he should present a copy of the arrest warrant, and his defenders were to protest that Barcaldine and his allies kept possession of it in order to delay the trial. If James, soon after being jailed, had managed to set the legal wheels rolling he would probably have been tried at the High Court in Edinburgh, where he might hope for a metropolitan jury of impartial minds. His unvisited confinement meant that the proceedings would be conducted at the circuit court in Inveraray, the shire capital. The prosecution lawyers were anxious that the little burgh should stage the drama. One of the solicitors for Glenure's relatives wrote: 'As to the trial I think it is now judged most proper to be carried on at Inveraray . . .'. Later in the same letter he expressed concern lest excessive slowness should thwart that purpose: ' . . . if it was delayed for this next circuit I'm afraid by running Letters they could force it to come on at Edr., before the circuit in the Spring.' At Inveraray most of the jurors would be Campbells, in a court which accepted simple majority verdicts. The previous circuit court held there had seen eight of that name sit on a jury of fifteen. The presiding judge might be the loftiest Campbell of all, the Duke of Argyll, if he chose to exercise his right as Lord Justice-General.

Towards the end of June Margaret's efforts to see her husband bore fruit. Having got a letter of instructions and copy of the 'wrongous imprisonment' Act from a sympathetic lawyer she sought the aid of Charles Stewart, the notary who had refused to act for James in the matter of the evictions for fear of offending the factor. She asked him to hand the copy of the Act to Colonel Crawfurd and demand a duplicate of the arrest warrant. Running true to form, the lawyer turned her down.

Margaret herself approached the colonel and he gave her leave to visit the prisoner. Whether she asked him for a copy of the arrest warrant is unrecorded, but she did not receive it. She was conducted to James's cell, accompanied by her two sisters. It is highly likely that at some point in her visit he asked her to urge the younger Ballachulish to approach Barcaldine for the vital docket. A week or two later she requested a second meeting with her husband. Crawfurd had in the meantime been transferred, and his successor not only rejected her petition on two occasions but threatened that if she did not leave Maryburgh she too would be imprisoned. Soon afterwards James was given permission to write to a friend for some requisites, and in the postscript took the opportunity to complain of his solitary confinement and other restrictions. The new governor furiously tossed the letter through the cell bars, vowing that if he did not rewrite it without the postscript he would not be allowed to pen another.

Shortly before Crawfurd was posted away from the fort young Ballachulish went to Glen Ure to speak to Barcaldine. Their acrid conversation was conducted on the bank of the river, probably because of a refusal by the Campbell to let Ballachulish enter Glenure House. The young man asked Barcaldine for the fair copy of the arrest warrant. He was told that he should solicit it from the jailer at Fort William, but that the matter was none of his business and if he pursued it further he would be pulled in and clapped in jail. Undeterred, Ballachulish travelled to Maryburgh, where he wrote to Crawfurd applying for a meeting with his tutor in the presence of any officer of the colonel's choosing. Crawfurd's adjutant wrote the reply: 'Sir, Colonel Crawfurd desires me to acquaint you, that you are represented to him as a person entirely in the confidence and secrets of Allan Breck Stewart; and that the intercourse you are said to have held with the supposed murderer of Glenure, at the time immediately preceding the murder, makes it (in his opinion) improper for your being admitted either to the prisoners, or as a friend into the garrison. The Colonel's illness he hopes will be an excuse for not writing himself.' On 6 July James was given a warrant copy from the Lord Justice-Clerk. The way was now open to engage legal assistance, but the official machinations to set the trial in Inveraray had attained their purpose.

The above narrative of these events is largely derived from *By-stander*, who must have gathered his information from some of the participants. It was vehemently contradicted in every particular by the writer of the *Justification*. He said that no private citizen had the authority to intervene in affairs of this nature, nor had it occurred in the case in point. He had recently spoken to Barcaldine, who denied ever receiving a letter from James demanding the arrest copy. (*By-stander* did not claim that he had; an unclear passage in his pamphlet was misunderstood.) With the exception of young Ballachulish, who was suspected of being an accessory to the crime, everyone who wished to confer with James was allowed to. It was common knowledge that Margaret went to bed with him. He was permitted to walk on the ramparts for two hours every day, a rare privilege for a prisoner in his position. Barcaldine's recollection of his riverbank interview with Ballachulish differed dramatically from the Stewart line. The laird's son did not so much as mention the warrant copy. He asked Barcaldine to release James into his custody under the terms of a bond of presentation. This was a written guarantee to deliver up the liberated prisoner to the holder of his arrest warrant at an agreed time and place for trial. Barcaldine replied that the crime was not bailable and the tacksman must be kept under lock and key until he faced a court. He warned the negotiator against dissuading people from telling all they knew about the murder, otherwise he, Barcaldine, must assume, as many others did, that he and his family were implicated in it. He listed several incidents that gave rise to suspicion: young Ballachulish was often closeted with James prior to the murder; he spent a considerable time alone with Breck two days before it happened; next day he left his home under the pretence of going to Inveraray but went to Aucharn instead; on that Wednesday night Breck slept in the same bedroom as old Ballachulish; and the laird met Glenure as he came off the ferry and walked chatting with him to the skirts of Lettermore Wood. Barcaldine told his visitor that when a few more facts were uncovered he would apply for a warrant to commit him to prison.

The accusation that the prosecutors resorted to underhand methods to site the trial in Inveraray was, said the *Justification*, 'extreamly jocular, tho Malicious and mean to the Last Degree'. In fact the original intention was to try the case in the Scottish capital but the proposal foundered in the face of strong objections. It was pointed out that anglophone jurors would not understand a word spoken by Gaelic-speaking witnesses and that the transportation of large numbers from Appin to Edinburgh could not be accomplished without huge expense.

Wherever the truth lay, the reality was that the sequestration of the chief prisoner inspired forebodings in his friends and a widening circle of well-wishers. To them, as well as to the agents of the law, the question of greatest moment was: where is Allan Breck? He seemed to hold the secret of James's innocence or guilt. Trial evidence was to relate that he made good speed east to his native Rannoch, where he spent a couple of days at his uncle's house. While there he came within an ace of being captured when a pair of his pursuers swooped on the place a bare two or three hours after he had left for Atholl. The last positive sighting took place towards the end of May. He asked the keeper of an alehouse for food and was given bread and cheese. On 28 May Breadalbane mentioned a rumour that the fugitive was heading for Menteith, on his way to England. As weeks passed the scope of the search broadened. Agents were dispersed throughout Argyll and beyond, and personal animosities among Jacobites were exploited in an effort to net the elusive soldier. Some Camerons lent a hand, certainly with divided emotions. All but the most bloody-minded abominated the killing of a defenceless rider shot from behind, a man who was the grandson of one of their greatest chiefs and the cousin of another. Lochaber teemed with investigators, and tavern whispers laid the murder at the door of unnamed Camerons who crossed the loch under cover of night to commit the deed outside their own territory.

Just as Glenure's relatives were convinced of a wide-ranging plot, so the Stewarts and their satellite families anxiously embraced what is nowadays informally known as the 'lone nutter' theory. They saw the danger to James, and the predictable harsh measures against themselves. Breaking the taciturn tradition of the Highlands they assured their questioners that Breck alone was guilty. Their insistence made Crawfurd even more suspicious. The astute governor had quickly calculated that Breck was being touted as an unaided assassin to draw the pack away from his adoptive father and others. Nevertheless it seemed clear that the absconder was a key operator in the tragedy, and his capture was vital. A month after his disappearance hopes of catching him were fading. The £200 reward stayed unclaimed, not surprisingly among a people who had spurned the £30 000 offered for the Young Pretender a few years before. Barcaldine wrote to the Lord Justice-Clerk requesting him to grant a pardon to Breck for his act of desertion. The defector could be a crucial witness in the case, he said. He also asked for a public proclamation that anyone who assisted the suspect to escape would be severely punished. Tinwald's reply was a model of mandarin politeness tinged with suppressed shock. To pardon a deserter without citing a reason would look very odd. To free him for the avowed purpose of giving evidence would look worse, especially to the jury. Barcaldine's best plan was to let Allan's friends know that if he gave himself up and told the truth influential people would mediate for him with certainty of success. As for imposing penalties on those who harboured the soldier, that lay only in the powers of the monarch and parliament. Nothing more was heard of Barcaldine's recommendations.

A dramatic development in mid July sent the hopes of the lawmen soaring. An army sergeant reported the capture near Carlisle of a man answering the description of Allan Breck.

'. . . he had on when apprehended by me Bleuish coat facd with black, Black Breeches, a Hatt and Feather Buff Coloured Wastcoat, a Red Waistcoat seen in the House when apprehended. He was pock-markd, about 5 feet 10 Inches high a little round shoulderd, & a little inkneed.'

4 Events Preceding the Trial

THE HUNTERS were filled with hope that their relentless quest had been rewarded. Writing in buoyant strain, Tinwald notified the Lords Justices, who forwarded the letter to the Duke of Newcastle in Hanover, who informed the king. Then a further bulletin on the captive chilled their exhilaration. He was five feet eleven inches, bore a great scar on his left cheek and was about twenty-two years old. Nevertheless there were enough points of resemblance to make it imperative to interview the man. Barcaldine's half-brother Robert wrote to say that Mungo was to make the journey to Carlisle 'As he knows Breck . . .'. The new factor did so, to find that the prisoner had satisfied his jailers that he was a sergeant in the Dutch army.

This incident, one of several in which sundry innocents were picked up, owes its significance to the fact that it discloses, through the adventitious survival of two letters, that Mungo knew Breck well enough to identify him. That fact helps to explain why the searchers clung so tenaciously to their conspiracy theory. It will be remembered that Mungo stated that the gunman he saw running up the hillside was so distant that he believed he could not possibly have fired the shot. Distance is a relative term. Even assuming that Mungo helped his uncle from his horse before starting up the brae in search of the killer, the runner could not have covered more than a hundred yards. The steepness of the hill – made steeper now by the construction of a forestry road twenty yards above the murder spot, when earth-moving machines deposited soil downhill – rule out the possibility that a man burdened with a musket could have sped farther. Mungo supplied another meaningful detail in a letter written shortly afterwards: 'I . . . saw the villain with a firelock in his hand, who on seeing me, though unarmed, made off without firing.' Plainly he saw the man's face, or that part of it revealed by a backward glance. If that face had been heavily pock-marked the fact would

57

have registered, however fleeting the exposure, and if the man had been tall, round-shouldered, strongly built, black-haired and knock-kneed, the lawyer would surely have noticed at least one of those characteristics. And if the runner was wearing a jacket and trousers that were too small for him might not that impression have struck the eye? If, in short, the escaper had been Allan Breck, Mungo, who knew him, would have identified him. His failure to name him must have been a sharp disappointment to his father. Barcaldine's instant conviction that James was the instigator would have been strengthened by the knowledge that it was Allan Breck who fled the scene. Any lingering hopes he may have entertained of proving that the fleeing figure was Breck were dashed when it emerged that Allan was wearing James's clothes on the day of the murder. Mungo could not conceivably have mistaken a black jacket and blue plaid trousers for a dun jacket and breeches of the same colour. There was immediate consolation in the discovery of the guns. It offered a possible direct link between the tacksman and the murder, as well as suggesting that the runaway had headed towards, or returned to, Aucharn. It chimed in with the countrywide belief that more than one marksman took flight from the wood. The disclosures brought into sharper focus three primary suspects – James, Allan Breck and the man in the dun clothes. The prevarications of some of the first persons to be questioned had the effect of assuring Barcaldine and his colleagues that there were many more in the plot.

In Edinburgh a groundswell of sympathy for James resulted in the opening of a public subscription to defray his legal expenses. A solicitor, Alexander Stewart of Edinglassie, agreed to act for him. He was a sharp-witted, combative bustler who, if he really was the pseudonymous *By-stander*, ranks high as a fiery pamphleteer. According to that source one of the first difficulties Edinglassie met was that of engaging skilled advocates, as many of the legal heavyweights had been retained in an advisory capacity by the prosecution, thereby denying their services to the defendant. Some lawyers were already committed to circuit court appearances and others were on summer holiday. Fear of the Duke of Argyll deterred several, while not a few demurred at the journey to Inveraray. It must be stressed here that the case against James was brought by dual prosecutors – the Crown, and Glenure's widow and children. It was the private prosecutors, in the persons of Barcaldine, his fellow peace officers and their lawyers, who were to be subjected to accusations of underhand dealing. Criticism of those who acted for the Crown was mainly limited to their conduct during the trial.

While Edinglassie made his preparations for the forensic battle ahead Barcaldine essayed a fresh, audacious ploy to clinch the case. He had been contacted by a distant relative, James Macgregor, a son of the storied Rob Roy. The Macgregors were so universally damned for their rogueries that the surname had been banned in an attempt to stamp out the tribe, and James now generally used the name of Drummond. Known as James More on account of his height, he was a skilled liar, adept at blending verifiable fact with profitable falsehood. But he had varnished the truth once or twice too often and was now generally regarded as a charlatan, a wolf in wolf's clothing. When Prince Charles Edward landed, the Macgregor approached the authorities and offered to arrest the Jacobite leaders. After the rebels' first successful skirmish with Government troops he hesitated, sniffing the wind for maximum advantage. The clans rose and the Highland Army headed south. James More joined it and fought at Prestonpans, where he claimed his thigh-bone was shattered. It is said that his clansmen carried him to the moor at Culloden in a litter, from which he roared his companies on to the charge. If true, the tale means that James More had the perhaps unique distinction of being stretchered *onto* a battlefield. With the rebellion in ruins he resumed his backstairs intercourse with the Government, receiving a pass from the Lord Justice-Clerk in 1747. Three years later he and his brother Robin entered the home of a teenage widow of ample means and carried off the screaming girl. They then induced a pliant clergyman to marry her to Robin. James More was pursued and arrested but his brother escaped. The widow contracted smallpox and died, but not before making judicial declarations acceptable to a court. From his prison cell James More let the Stirlingshire lawmen know that if they managed to defer his trial his friends would track down Glenure's killers. The officers reported the offer to the Lord Advocate, who insisted on pressing on with the full rigour of the law, confident that it was the best method to force the Macgregors to smoke out the plotters. Only when they had done so, he ruled, would it be time to consider mitigation of punishment. James More was put on trial for what was then a capital offence and the jury returned a verdict of guilty on the kidnap charge. But, they added, his guilt was diminished by the widow's subsequent acquiescence to the marriage. They found the charges of forcible marriage and rape not proven. Eleven jurors signed a letter to the presiding judge, Tinwald, stating that they did not wish to see James More hanged. Tinwald ordered counsel for both sides to submit final arguments in writing, and he set the date for sentencing as 20 November. Macgregor was lodged in Edinburgh's tolbooth to brood on the prospect of a one-way excursion to the scaffold.

The resourceful knave was not the man to await the decision with Socratic resignation. He got in touch with Barcaldine and offered him a meaty piece of testimony against the tacksman. James Stewart had visited him in jail when he journeyed to Edinburgh to apply for the injunction, and the resulting interview formed the substance of the evidence the Macgregor proposed to give. According to the *Justification* James of the Glen asked a prisoner who was locked up with James More to remove himself so that he could have a private talk with his cellmate. An unsigned record of what passed between the two Jameses lies in the John McGregor Collection in the Scottish Record Office. Its title is *Copie of a Conversation that past Betwixt James Stewart Tacksman of Acharn in Appin & James Drummond Prisoner at Edinburgh in April 1752.* The Stewart vilified the Barcaldine

Campbells who, he asserted, 'woud take their advantage of mankind'. He assailed his own chief, Appin, describing him as a scoundrel, for selling property in Glen Duror worth five hundred pounds to Glenure. Before long the man would have handed over his entire estate. Appin must be bewitched to have dealings with people who would like to cut his throat. As for Red Colin, 'I woud think no more sin to shoot such a monster than I woud think of taking that Dram that lays before us,' and '. . . such a monster as this man (meaning Glenure) shoud not live among Christians.' James then suggested that James More should give him a letter for his brother Robin instructing him to shoot Glenure with a very good gun supplied by the tacksman. The killer's reward would be enough money to transport him to France, where Ardsheal's influence could obtain for him an army commission or a pension, whichever he preferred. James More's good offices would earn him the lease of a piece of land which the tacksman hoped to induce young Ballachulish to make over to him. The Macgregor refused to have anything to do with the scheme and advised his visitor to do likewise. James consented to drop it, cautioning the prisoner not to breathe a word of the proposal.

Such was the remarkable story Barcaldine received from the villain. With it came a guarantee to swear to its truth in exchange for a pardon on the abduction charge. Barcaldine drew up a memorial to the Barons of Exchequer summarising the state of the investigation, regretting that the evidence was not yet conclusive, and relating James More's account. He made the point that nothing less than a pardon could enable the convict to testify against James, who was the mainspring of the plot. Requesting that the Barons forward the memorial to the Lords Justices, he ended bluntly by reminding them that his brother had laid down his life in their service. The petition was sent to Pelham on 12 August with a covering letter signed by two Barons, one of whom was the Lord Chief, a torpid placeman named Idle. They declared their support for the memorial, 'Being perswaded, That it will be greatly for the service to the publick, That James Stewart mentioned in the Memorial herewith sent, be convicted . . .'

While Barcaldine was composing the document the Lord Advocate, William Grant of Prestongrange, was putting the finishing touches to his 'criminal libel' against James. Prestongrange had attained the highest prosecuting legal office in the difficult year of 1746. Like most Scots in positions of power he opposed harsh measures against former rebels. As MP for the Elgin Burghs he spoke for the abolition of heritable jurisdictions, a measure he considered essential if the country was to enjoy an enduring peace. The post of Lord Advocate made him not only Scotland's chief prosecutor but in practice the head of its Administration. Prestongrange's reputation for rectitude was rather more than the usual coronet of compliments with which lawyers of the period by an unspoken code laurelled each other. Later historians have echoed the tributes of his contemporaries, though some disapproved of his conduct in the Glenure case. Since assuming office he had never actively appeared in a circuit court, nor had any of his four immediate predecessors. On this occasion, he said, he was resolved to make an exception and lead for the Crown in view of the national importance of the issue. He had been incensed by reports from London that the Scottish legal authorities could not be relied on to prosecute James More Macgregor Drummond with vigour, and that a panel of Scots would refuse to reach a guilty verdict against James of the Glen. He let fly an angry letter to Hardwicke protesting that 'an Argyleshire Jury may be found, as ready to convict the murderers of a Campbell, as any Jury, in Middlesex, or Mid-lothian would be . . .'. The Advocate's motive in conducting the case personally may not have been as high-minded as he affected. It was he who had introduced the Annexing Bill in the House of Commons a few months previously, and he may have felt, as others did, that the murder was a prompt and unequivocal response to it.

The law decreed that the criminal libel – in modern usage,

the charge or charges against the defendant – should be detailed and accurate, a requirement that tended to inspire narratives of extreme length. In this case the charge ran to more than 4500 words, or about 12 pages of this book. As the defence counsel were not at the time permitted to see the precognitions on which the indictment was based they considered it vital to study the document at the earliest moment. While it was being printed Edinglassie asked one of the solicitors for the prosecution if he could have a copy. The request was rejected, in breach of customary professional courtesy. *By-stander* wrote that 'a person of great distinction was threatened with a complaint against him, if he, in compassion, to which he was much inclined, should give or order a copy for the pannel's (defendant's) agent.' That person may well have been the Lord Advocate. The refusal of the opposition agent to furnish a copy of the indictment shortened the time available to prepare a defence. The papers would be served on the accused in Fort William, with a consequent loss of three days while they were rushed back to Edinburgh. By the third week of August Edinglassie found himself gravely unready. The trial was scheduled to begin on 21 September, but a cruel trick of circumstances curtailed the five-week period of preparation he would have enjoyed in any year but 1752. In the previous year an Act had been passed adopting the Gregorian calendar. One of its provisions was that eleven days should be excised from September 1752. Thus the second day of that month was to be followed by the fourteenth in the new style, an adjustment that deleted irreplaceable time. Then a copy of the indictment fell into Edinglassie's hands through an incident that reads like an implausible flight of fancy by a tired novelist. When the printers had run off their copies they broke up the type to prevent leaks. They overlooked a galley proof that someone had dropped on the floor. It was picked up by a casual visitor – if indeed that is what he was – and brought to the defence agent. The private prosecutors started legal proceedings against the visitor, but dropped them on being advised that it would not be wise.

Edinglassie read the lengthy indictment with dismay. James and Allan Breck were charged with being 'guilty, actors, or art and part of the said heinous crime of murder . . .'. 'Art and part' was a term roughly corresponding to 'accessory' in the English system. The charge went on to specify that Allan fired the shot and the older man was his collaborator. The direct evidence against them was 'scrimp', to quote Barcaldine's assessment of it, and it was clear that the prosecution intended to rely heavily on the threats breathed by the two accused. Edinglassie despairingly noted that these threats were mentioned only in the most general terms; neither names of witnesses, dates or places were supplied. This essential part of the testimony was to be disclosed in the course of the trial, like batteries unmasked on a battlefield, when it was too late to investigate and confute it.

So depressed was the solicitor over James's prospects that he seriously considered giving up the case and advising him to plead for himself. That course bristled with uncertainties, so he decided to consult 'one of the first counsel against him', as *By-stander* discreetly put it. It is more than possible that the man whose advice he sought was Prestongrange. At the trial one of the advocates eventually hired for the defence gracefully acknowledged that it was the Lord Advocate who had prevailed on him and others to enter the lists. It may well have been a visit from Edinglassie that prompted Prestongrange to use his influence for the benefit of the adversaries. What is certain is that the lawyer the defence agent conferred with pressed him not to abandon his cause. Edinglassie took the advice and successfully completed his team within a week or so. It comprised two sheriffs, George Brown of Forfar and Thomas Miller of Kirkcudbright, and two younger men in their middle or late twenties, Walter Stewart and Robert Macintosh. The busy agent next determined to hurry to Fort William for a long overdue conference with his client. What was even more fundamentally necessary was to question the other prisoners, whose evidence would decisively affect the verdict.

No effort had been made to secure the freedom of those unfortunates although their imprisonment was arguably more unlawful than that of James. Not merely were they detained without a warrant but they were held in a military building which, while legally it could house suspected offenders, could not be used to hold witnesses. A few days after James's arrest Colonel Crawfurd, in a letter to his commander-in-chief, set down his method of extracting information from close-mouthed Highlanders. His secret was to play without scruple on their fears, affections and hostilities 'when my intentions were, that their disscoverys (disclosures) shou'd produce a general good . . .'. He segregated all the main witnesses as a precaution against collusion. For three months James's servants John Beg and Dugald were shackled or handcuffed. As has been mentioned, his tactic of first confining John Beg with a condemned man and then proffering a bribe paid dividends in the unearthing of the muskets. James was to level the accusation that Ballachulish's herdsman was promised a hundred pounds if his evidence proved useful. The eighteen-year old farm-hand teased his captors by first telling them that the fishing-rod he lent Allan Breck lacked a hook, then later adding that Breck attached one and caught fish. Crawfurd employed another ancient snare by installing his own man in the cell with the two Maccolls. The spy, who was awaiting trial on a theft charge, reported that one of the labourers told him that Allan Oig was the man who had been with Breck at the time of the murder, and that Dugald said he saw Allan Oig and a young Stewart neighbour walk towards the wood that day. Both Maccolls were described as believing that young Allan would swing with his father. The informer was released without trial. His name appeared on the list of prosecution witnesses but he was not called.

When John Don handed over James's clothes in the middle of July the main prisoners faced a further grilling. The powder-horn found in a pocket was of cardinal relevance for two obvious reasons: it showed that Allan Breck was equipped for shooting, and if it could be proved that the horn belonged to James his defence would be appreciably weakened. John Beg and Dugald were interrogated more than once and denied that it came from Aucharn. Crawfurd, who had by this time been posted from the fort, wrote to recommend that James, Allan Oig and William the merchant be questioned about it. Although there is no surviving scrap of paper to indicate that the suggestion was carried out it seems safe to conclude that it was, and the answers were in the negative.

At about the same time Barcaldine was urged by his half-brother Sheriff Duncan to send some, if not all, of the detainees to Inveraray. Duncan argued that it was impossible to prevent so many prisoners from communicating with each other in such a confined space. Besides, the first one to be sent to the Campbell capital would look on himself as 'a gon man', which might have the effect of jogging his memory along productive paths. Dugald was a salient choice, he said, for as well as being the most vulnerable he knew as much of the affair as any of the other servants. Barcaldine turned down his brother's plan. On 3 August, however, two prisoners were escorted to Inveraray, but their identities are not known.

Later that month young Ballachulish went to Edinburgh to confer with Edinglassie and the defence advocates. No doubt he told the solicitor what he knew of events at the fort. Edinglassie penned a petition, quoting the 1701 Act, requesting access to James, his sons Allan Oig and Charles, the servants John Beg and Dugald, Sandy Bane, John Don and John Carmichael. The Lord Justice-Clerk, to whom it was directed, invited him to an interview and asked if he had received written instructions to act for any or all of the prisoners. Edinglassie replied that he had been given a letter from James authorising him to proceed on behalf of himself and the other inmates, but had no direct orders from the men themselves. Tinwald asked to see the letter but the agent declined to show it on the grounds that it contained material he preferred not to reveal for the moment. He offered to swear on oath that it set out the mandates he claimed. The offer was turned down. Tinwald responded to the petition by issuing a warrant requiring the jailers at Fort William to allow visits to James by his lawyers and friends. It refused access to the other detainees because they had not given individually written instructions. Edinglassie's rage at this decision is recorded in a spatter of furious italics in *By-stander*'s comments. The Lord Justice-Clerk *'recommends'* admittance to James. He prohibits access to the other prisoners 'where *they are said* to be confined . . .'. Those men were being held incommunicado because they had not instructed a lawyer, and they could not instruct a lawyer because they were being held incommunicado. Though frustrated and disappointed, Edinglassie sent the warrant express to the fort.

On the next day, 21 August, before the directive arrived, criminal letters were served on James in his cell. A few days later they were proclaimed against Allan Breck at Aucharn and Inveraray. One effect of the presentation of the indictment was to render superfluous the warrant Tinwald had so grudgingly conceded: by legal right a prisoner who had been served with a charge was entitled to advise with his agent to a reasonable degree. For this reason the permit so contentiously won was a dead letter before it reached its destination. But the letter of the law had been observed by granting the defence nineteen days to construct their case; only fifteen were obligatory. However, three of the remaining days were Sundays, when no business could be conducted for sabbatarian reasons, so the total was reduced to sixteen. From those sixteen must be deducted four for James's journey to Inveraray with a military guard, leaving twelve days to devise a strategy to save him from the gibbet. Swiftly setting in motion what measures he could take in the capital, Edinglassie set out for Fort William on 31 August.

Two days later he reached Tyndrum, a sleepy crossroads settlement cradled among noble peaks. He there encountered a party of soldiers escorting James en route. He asked the officer-in-charge if he could hold a roadside consultation with his client.

The soldier was understandably reluctant, for he had his orders. Edinglassie brandished a copy of the warrant giving him leave to converse with the prisoner. The officer pointed out that it was addressed to the jailers and commander at the fort, and was therefore framed to be put into effect there. A lengthy discussion ensued. The lawyer was convinced that the prosecution had contrived James's removal to Inveraray to prevent a meeting between defendant and defender, and may even have told the officer so. Finally the military man relented and allowed the two Stewarts to discuss their business. By this unpredictable turn of events Edinglassie gained the consultation he so urgently needed. It lasted about an hour. Then the redcoats continued on their way with the prisoner and the lawyer hurried on to Appin. He learned that the Campbells, attended by a squad from the fort, had three times descended on Aucharn and gone through the tacksman's papers, on each occasion without a warrant. They took away any items they thought would prove useful, including Allan Oig's disputed letter in which he vowed that Glen Duror would cost Glenure and Ballieveolan dear. Edinglassie managed to salvage five letters from the factor to James which ranged in tone from civil to cordial. During his busy few days in Appin the changeover to the Gregorian calendar advanced the opening of the trial by the prescribed eleven days. By the time he hastened to Inveraray on 18 September, as it was newly styled, there were fewer than seventy-two hours left. That evening he talked with some of the defence advocates. An immediate interview with James being of pivotal importance, they applied to the jailer, who responded that no one was permitted to see the prisoner without the written consent of the Duke of Argyll. The lawyers drew up a petition to be presented to His Grace the next morning. Then a message arrived from the duke granting a meeting. In the following forenoon, less than two days before the trial opening, the defence team met for the first time the man whose life depended on their skill.

James's fellow prisoners had reached the trim town before

Edinglassie. With other key witnesses they were put up in the tolbooth, where the turnkeys ruled out any communion among them by installing two narks in each cell. John Don was by now co-operating wholeheartedly with the prosecutors. Katharine the dairymaid, who was compelled to share a cell with him, told him that on the day of the murder she hid Allan Breck's clothes on the brae, as instructed by Margaret. She retrieved them next day, also on the orders of her mistress. John Don passed on this admission to the investigators, promising to work on the prisoners to tell all they knew. James's oldest farm labourer, John More, who had by this time left his employ, accepted a bribe from Stonefield's son, giving him to understand that he would affirm that his former master had sent to France for Breck. Sandy Bane stubbornly told him that he stood by his June declaration in every detail. Young Stonefield let Barcaldine know that he intended to precognose the central witnesses again, with high hopes of new discoveries.

The Lord Advocate went to Inveraray on the eve of the trial, Wednesday, 20 September. There he received a letter addressed to the chief Baron and his colleague which they had forwarded from Edinburgh. It was a reply from the Lords Justices to the covering letter the Barons had sent approving Barcaldine's memorial which called for a pardon for James More Drummond. Their Lordships expressed themselves at some length and with diplomatic finesse. They were 'extremely desirous that the Several Persons concerned in the Infamous Murder . . . should be brought to condign Punishment and particularly that James Stewart of Aucharn, who is now in Custody, and is to be tryed at the ensuing Circuit at Inveraray, for contriving and abetting that Horrid Crime, should not escape the Judgment of the Law, for want of evidence.' They pointed out that James More had been involved in serious crimes, possibly including the murder of Colin Campbell. They would not support the plea contained in the memorial as there as not sufficient time before the trial to obtain a royal pardon. The letter was dated 14 September, when the king was still on his extended holiday in Hanover.

The news of a memorial came as a complete surprise to the Lord Advocate. When Barcaldine and the Barons had sent it to London he was not informed, let alone consulted. He later signed a list of prosecution witnesses drawn up by Glenure's kin. Because of its length he added his signature without scanning the 151 names. Number 128 was James Drummond *alias* Macgregor *alias* James More. The Campbells had inserted the name in the hope that a pardon would be granted in time to allow him to testify. Prestongrange now sent for Barcaldine and let him know the contents of the Lords Justices' letter. He spelled out the alternatives. The trial could proceed as planned without the evidence of James More, or it could be postponed until after the king had given his decision on the pardon. Without hesitation Barcaldine asked that the legal process go ahead at Inveraray, surmising that the prosecution would lose more by deferring the trial than it would gain by James More's testimony, in the highly speculative event of his being set free. What Barcaldine had in mind is not difficult to guess. They would lose the precious advantage of having a thoroughly prepared brief to pit against a defence cobbled together at the last minute. Even more crucially they would forfeit a Campbell jury in a court presided over by the chief of the breed.

In a display of uncertainty surprising in the country's highest prosecutor Prestongrange canvassed the opinions of knowledgeable associates. He met considerable scepticism about James More's willingness to send a fellow veteran of the Rising to the scaffold once he had pocketed his pardon. Serious doubts were voiced as to whether an Edinburgh jury would believe such a man. In the light of these sensible observations the Advocate made up his mind that the trial should proceed as scheduled. He communicated his decision to Barcaldine, who expressed complete satisfaction. James More's astonishing account was never narrated in open court but *By-stander* accused him of sending a written résumé of his conversation with the defendant to Inveraray, where one of the prosecution advocates used information derived from it. The author reported a rumour that the statement was handed around the jury. Undeniably the Macgregor's story gained currency during the trial, possibly through the mouth of Colin Campbell of Carwhin, one of the peace officers engaged in the precognitions who was chosen as a juror, and it surfaced briefly, though obliquely, in a prosecution speech, as will become apparent.

5 The Trial: Day 1

INVERARAY WAS A neat, pretty centre with half a thousand inhabitants. It was proud of its royal burgh status, even if the charter bore the signature of a Stuart king, Charles I. Whitewashed cottages predominated, but around the market cross stood many stone-built houses roofed with slate, some rising to two storeys. There were a couple of schools, a snug inn, a generous sprinkling of taverns and a 'double' church, steepled and bell-towered, where worshippers could choose to hear a sermon preached in English or Gaelic. A twin-arched bridge spanned the River Aray not far from where it glides into Loch Fyne, whose rich herring shoals provided the town's sole industry and its pervading reek. At a little distance the ancestral castle of the clan chiefs crumbled into dilapidation while its Gothic successor rose in blue-grey stone to a grandeur that was to draw from Dr Johnson the exclamation: 'What I admire here is the total defiance of expense.' In addition to hosting meetings of the Commissioners of Supply the busy seat of adminstration housed various types of tribunal – Admiralty, sheriff's and circuit court – and was consequently peopled by a sizeable resident community of black-gowned legal officers. Parchments signed in the tolbooth touched the lives of all who dwelt in Argyll, eight thousand square miles of mountains, lochs and islands.

The hereditary potentate was Archibald, the seventy-year old Duke of Argyll. Educated at Eton, Glasgow University and Utrecht, he immersed himself in politics as a young man and sat on the commission which was set up to shape the Act of Union. During the 1715 rebellion he commanded the Inveraray garrison when the burgh was menaced by a considerable force that included the Stewarts of Appin, and he fought at Sheriffmuir, where he collected a leg-wound that left him permanently lame. With his brother John, the second duke, he virtually ruled Scotland throughout more than two decades of Walpole's second administration. At the beginning of the 'Forty-five he returned to London, giving as reason that his advice was more valuable to the Government than his presence in Scotland. His enemies, not all of them Jacobites, branded the move as a ruse to demonstrate to both sides that he was not in arms against them. After Culloden he came back to Scotland and used his immense influence to curb the depredations of the Duke of Cumberland's men. This did not imply any sympathy towards the Stuart cause, as he was a committed supporter of the ruling family. To expect a man of his stamp to deal even-handedly with James Stewart would have been the zenith of optimism. When some of his acolytes asked him how the defence lawyers were to be lodged he pierced them with a glacial scowl and told them not to bother him with such matters. The office of Lord Justice General, which Argyll had held for more than forty years, was by this time largely ceremonial but still carried the privilege of acting as presiding judge at circuit courts. The duke was an occasional attender, usually limiting his participation to opening formally the court's business, but at this sederunt he occupied the chair for most of the trial. Sharing the bench with him were two Lords of Justiciary, Elchies and Kilkerran. In view of the hundreds of spectators anticipated and the cramped and decrepit state of the existing courtroom Stonefield decided to hold the proceedings in the church. This was a single chamber divided in two by a central partition. One half was the Lowland or English Church and the other housed the Highland, Gaelic-speaking congregation. The sheriff chose the English compartment. Its internal floor space was a rectangle fifty-four feet by twenty, an area slightly larger than a modern badminton court. Two galleries on opposite walls doubtless played their part in accommodating the throngs.

At six o'clock in the morning on Thursday, 21 September, while the church bell tolled reveille, the session opened. The assizers – the panel from whose numbers a jury might be selected – were called, and all but four answered to their names. One of these was Appin, who had written to Barcaldine explaining that his daughter Anne, an only child, was ill. Another was a man who was unfit to travel. Each of the three fit absentees was fined five pounds eleven shillings. The first case listed for decision was that of a woman accused of murdering a child, presumably her own, but it was postponed until the following Monday to make way for the main event, so to say. Allan Breck was ritually summoned to court by the mace-bearer and, on failing to appear, pronounced an outlaw. Then the indictment was read. Surprisingly, it contained no reference to Mungo's having seen the fleeing gunman, or the ferryman's noticing Breck near the south slip around lunchtime on the murder day. The indictment concluded by claiming that its version of events would be proved. The prosecution would substantiate the defendant's death threats, and certain exhibits and writings complete their case that the accused were 'guilty, actors, or art and part of the said murder'. Shackled and flanked by guards, James was asked how he pleaded. He replied, 'My Lords, I am not guilty of the crime of which I am accused, and I refer to my lawyers to make my defence.' Their first line of defence was to raise 'a plea in bar of trial'. This was to be an appeal to abort the proceedings on the grounds that a person accused of being an accessory to a crime could not be tried before the principal. The court therefore embarked on a debate on 'the relevancy of the libel' – in broad modern terms, whether there was a case to answer. This decision would be handed down by the two junior judges, with the Lord Justice-General holding a casting vote if they should disagree. No verbatim account of the circuit sitting exists, as there were no shorthand writers present, but a book of the trial was published in 1753. It contains the speeches of counsel, reconstructed by them from their notes, and the summaries of oral evidence inscribed in the West Circuit Book. All the documentary evidence, including the judicial declarations of the tacksman and his family, was printed. Missing were a few official papers, a draft letter by James, and a draft instrument of protest against the evictions.

Mr Walter Stewart made the opening speech for the defence.

He expressed horror at the brutality of the crime, condemned what he saw as a whispering campaign against his client and appealed for a fair hearing. He declared his faith in James's innocence. The prosecutors had violated the man's legal rights by isolating him for months in defiance of the wrongful imprisonment Act, searching his house without a warrant and producing in court written declarations by his wife and children. In addition to these transgressions the defence had been denied the services of many experienced advocates, and Argyll himself had delayed James's access to his lawyers at Inveraray.

The counsel then traced the course of the relations between Glenure and his sub-factor. He stressed that on the day of the murder James was still pursuing a legal solution. He had nothing to lose by the ejections, being unrelated to any of the tenants. Their removal would not be prevented by Glenure's death, which would have the effect of cancelling the gentleman's agreement that allowed him to raise 'second rents'. The tacksman's reputation as a kindly and peace-loving man who at that very time was rearing several orphans made assassination unimaginable.

The opposition must prove that Allan Breck fired the shot, or the case against James collapsed. On the Monday the conspiracy was allegedly hatched they were alone together merely for as long as it took them to walk fifty yards. During the outlaw's Highland visits he often laid aside his uniform and borrowed clothes from his friends. Who could possibly believe that James gave Allan his own clothes *four* days before the murder? The asseveration that the defendant displayed unconcern when told of the slaying was false; he sent some of his family and friends to assist with the corpse.

The defence advocate then narrated an incident that must have come as a shock to his opponents. On the morning after the crime Donald Stewart, a nephew and son-in-law of old Ballachulish, told James that he had met Allan Breck in the fields about nine o'clock the previous evening. Breck told him that he was going to Caolasnacon and asked him to entreat James to forward him money there. It was in response to this message that his client sent Sandy Bane to William a little later. This story knocked away one of the main props of the prosecution case – that James knew where to send the cash without being told. The surprise, and suspicion, must have been all the more complete as Donald had made a precognition in which he said nothing of a sunset meeting with the outlaw.

Of the indictment's version of what passed between John Don and Allan Breck, Stewart continued, he would merely say that it was affirmable by only one person, and would be hearsay evidence, and therefore inadmissable. The defendant sent his foster-son cash in an instinctive impulse to save him from military justice. On learning that Breck was a leading suspect he instantly 'papered' him in an effort to secure his arrest. James behaved honourably, acting only as any member of the court would have done in his position. (At this point Argyll reproved the speaker for claiming that he or his brother judges would have taken the course the accused had. James turned to one of his agents and said, 'You may do for me what you will; but I know my fate by what the Duke of Argyll has just said to Mr Stewart.')

The advocate resumed by strenuously contending that the accessory to a crime should not be tried before the principal. It could result in a guilty verdict against an absent defendant, a breach of a fundamental principle of law. Before an accessory could be convicted his confederate must be proved to have performed the act. Otherwise an absent principal's enemies could testify against him, and witnesses capable of exonerating him go unheard. English law required that the chief malefactor be tried first. The law of Scotland took the same stance, backed by the written opinion of the great seventeenth-century jurist, Sir George Mackenzie.

Even if all the facts alleged could be proved, Stewart concluded, they were 'so extremely vague and trivial' that they could not even direct suspicion towards his client, let alone convict him. He asked their Lordships to decide that there was no case to answer.

76

If they should rule against the plea he requested that evidence be heard. His final remarks were addressed to the assizers. The more savage the crime the more conclusive must be the proof. If they were certain of the accused's guilt they must bring in such a judgment but they must also keep it in their eye that it was better that twenty guilty men escape than one innocent man die by their verdict.

Mr Robert Macintosh spoke next for the defence. His speech rang with rhetorical flourishes and soaring hyperboles, as when he described the crime as 'assassination in face of the sun'. He began by avowing his horror at the death of Glenure, whose friend he was. To the number of legal obstacles which Mr Stewart had deplored he added another, that witnesses had been imprisoned, and only the private prosecutors and their agents permitted to see them. He absolved the public prosecutor, Prestongrange, of blame, laying it unequivocally at the door of Glenure's relatives. He saw no disadvantage to his client in being tried at Inveraray, where the duke's presence ensured impartiality, but warned the assizers against prejudice. Prejudice was like a jaundiced eye applied to a magnifying glass; it saw everything yellow and enlarged.

Macintosh re-stated the objection to trying the accomplice before the perpetrator. To convict James the prosecution must establish beyond doubt that Allan Breck fired the shot, yet the facts set out in the indictment did not begin to amount to that conclusion. The opposition must explain away James's good reputation and untarnished private life. (A traditional tale relates that Argyll interjected that no man who rebelled against his king could be in high esteem, to which Macintosh retorted that it would be difficult to tell how many Argylls had rebelled. The duke's grandfather and great-grandfather had been executed for high treason.) Even if the fact did prove Breck guilty – even, indeed, if the outlaw were present in court and confessed – nothing detrimental to his client's innocence could be inferred. That innocence was called in question by a bare two items in the indictment, the clothing and the money. The defence would show that Allan often changed his apparel and that James knew where to send the guineas as the result of a message from the soldier. If, when he sent the money, he knew Allan to be the murderer it was a wrong action, possibly punishable by law, but it did not make him an accessory. The accused had despatched the cash out of natural concern for his ward, fearing that if the military caught him a courtmartial would make short work of him, thereby saving their Lordships the trouble of trying him.

Macintosh too dismissed the stockman's story. It was one man's recital of a conversation with another. All rules of evidence forbade hearsay, and on this occasion the reported remarks were uttered by the very man who was accused of the deed. If Allan Breck really did throw suspicion on James and his son his reason may have been to deflect attention from his guilty self. As for the allegation that his client showed no dismay at Glenure's death, it was neither true nor evidence. Besides, an immoderate display of grief would have been much more undeserving of belief. The only remnant of the indictment that remained to be disposed of was the death threats, but as they had not been specified he could not comment on them, nor could the defence refute them unless they were related in evidence.

The type of testimony against James reminded him of the monstrous machine designed by an inventor to wreak havoc among his country's enemies. He took his plans to his leader, who ordered him to destroy them lest the terrible device should be used against themselves. The evidence adduced to convict this defendant could not be anything but circumstantial. This, he conceded, could be as conclusive as direct depositions by eyewitnesses. People might lie or be mistaken, but facts were unbending. However, each circumstance in the chain of proof must be unarguable, and a missing link spelt failure. The more serious the crime the more decisive must be the proof. In the present instance 'it would almost require to see the blood of the innocent reeking on the hands of the guilty'.

In a short peroration touched with sober resignation the lawyer reminded his listeners that James was on trial for his life, and that he insisted that his hands were clean. If his plea were to fail, his death should be seen as a sacrifice to the rule of law, the last act in the nation's blood-letting, and not the revenge of the murdered man's friends or a sop to ignorant prejudice.

Mr Simon Fraser, counsel for the private prosecutors, was a shrewd choice. At the age of nineteen he had led his clan in the cause of the Stuarts. He escaped the fate of his double-dealing father, Lord Lovat, whose head had tumbled on Tower Hill, and after a year's imprisonment qualified for the bar. Now deprived of lands and title, his first appearance as an advocate was against a comrade-in-arms. James was to find himself assailed with what Oscar Wilde, when in a faintly similar plight, noted as 'all the added bitterness of an old friend'. Fraser led off with a by now ritual expression of repugnance at the killing. This trial was important not only in its implications for the safety of individuals but also for the very nation itself. It was 'the most daring and barefaced insult to be offered to His Majesty's authority and Government, and offered at a time when we, in common with His Majesty's other subjects, are enjoying the fruits of his most benign reign.' The world must be shown that the murder had been the work of one or two wicked men, and that they had not gone unpunished.

He gave a brief version of the incidents that led to the trial. As a natural brother of Ardsheal, who had led the Appin Stewarts in the 'Forty-five, James became his family's *de facto* leader. His early resentment at the appointment of Red Colin to the factorship turned to hatred when he was evicted. The success of Glenure in overturning the suspension order enraged him to the point of murder. He assembled different groups of men he could trust, denounced the factor, and promised that he would reward anyone who had nerve enough to kill him, a safe passage to France and a solid pension. (Here was unmistakable proof that Fraser had been informed of the defendant's talk with

James More Drummond. No evidence was to be given that the tacksman offered anyone anything.) Then came Allan Breck, a wild deserter precisely suited to James's design. They agreed the basic plan that Breck should fire the shot and James ensure his escape. Even then their loathing for Glenure was such that they could not control their outcries. Both issued repeated menaces. Allan said he would shoot his man at the first opportunity and his foster-father stated that he would do the same even if he were so crippled as to have to drag himself to a window. Allan spent the weekend before the murder at Fasnacloich House, near Glenure's residence, in order to spy on the factor's movements. There he learned that Glenure had brought the eviction orders and aimed to enforce them. On observing his quarry leave for Fort William he hurried to Aucharn and told James the news. They settled the details and the tacksman gave Breck his workaday clothes, the better to merge with his surroundings. As a means of cloaking his purpose the assassin whiled away the succeeding two days paying calls on his friends at Ballachulish, Glencoe and Callert, all places within easy walking distance of the ferry by which Glenure must return.

Fraser's account of the events leading up to and ensuing after the murder tallied closely with that of the indictment. He mentioned the incident unpredictably omitted from it, Breck's encounter with the ferryman. He related that the defector hastily called the boatman aside a few hours before the slaying and 'inquired, with more than ordinary earnestness and anxiety, if Glenure had passed there that day, and being answered that he had not, Allan immediately ran up the hill towards the high ground above the house . . .'. (This may have come as a blow to the defence. They almost certainly knew that the ferryman would testify that he had seen the outlaw at the slip, but they may have been unaware that he would report a damaging conversation with him. In his precognition the ferryman had said that he *saw* Breck at about lunchtime.)

Fraser filled out the indictment's summary of the dialogue

between John Don and Allan Breck. He quoted the stockman as saying that the fugitive told him that James and Allan Oig would be safe if they could control their tongues, especially the son's, for he was more free-spoken than his father. The young advocate explained the tacksman's refusal to attend the corpse as due to concern, not for the luckless victim but the barbarous killer.

The opening defence counsel had protested that the facts were trivial, but conspiracy by its secret nature yielded few certainties. An unbroken chain of circumstances formed the case for the prosecution. First came growing resentment, next violent threats, finally the murder. The killer's movements were tracked from place to place and day to day, almost to the very scene of the outrage. That his collaborator knew where to send him the guineas and clothes, plainly by prior arrangement, was a point of the utmost significance.

The objection to trying the accessory before the principal could not be allowed to stand. Such defects as existed in the current practice were trifling compared with those that would flow from a ruling that the principal must be tried first. It would prohibit the trial of any accessory if his guilty partner went on the run. It would permit any villain to hire another to commit a crime, send him somewhere safe, and laugh at the law.

Exception had been taken to the inclusion among the Crown exhibits of the judicial declarations of the defendant's wife and children, who could not legally be called as witnesses against him. Those statements had been taken at an early stage in the investigation when everyone in the area was being examined and no particular person charged with the crime. If the declarations were to be read at a jury trial it would be solely to prove that the declarants made certain affirmations, and not to establish the truth or otherwise of the statements themselves. If James's family had made incriminating remarks about him in the presence of witnesses, those witnesses could have been called in evidence. Producing the family's judicially attested written statements amounted to the same thing.

The complaint that the accused was kept in solitary confinement is explained by his imprisonment in a military jail. The governor applied the rules laid down for state prisoners, not common criminals, with whom he was less familiar. When the difference in the prescribed treatment was explained to him he instantly complied, and admission was allowed at once. Unfortunately he was transferred and his successor also innocently imposed the strict code for state detainees. As soon as the law was expounded to him he obeyed it. As for the delay in admitting the defence lawyers to James in Inveraray, it lasted less than an hour. Sheriff Stonefield, declining to allow a meeting without the duke's approval, sent for his authorisation, which was given forthwith. The charge that the prosecution had snapped up all the ablest lawyers could not be upheld after a glance at the two teams; the defence held the lead in age and experience if one excepted from the equation the Lord Advocate, whose office obliged him to appear for the Crown.

Fraser ended by appealing to the judges to rule in favour of a trial by jury. He enjoined the assizers to discriminate carefully between their natural abhorrence of the murder and any personal animus against the defendant, whom they owed an unprejudiced examination of the evidence to decide his innocence or guilt.

Opening for the Crown, Mr James Erskine, sheriff-depute of Perthshire, declared that he would confine his speech to refuting the arguments put forward by the other side. Much of their case consisted of indignant accusations of 'unfair advantages and unlawful oppression upon the part of the prosecutors'. Even if this were true – which it was not – it would be no defence to the charge. The claim that James was deprived of the best pleaders was disproved by the high abilities of the very gentlemen who made it. No law was infringed in the course of the accused's imprisonment. As a person suspected of a capital crime he was kept in secure detention without any breach of the Act pertaining to wrongful confinement. The magistrates barred any visitor who did not have a warrant because James succeeded in sending messages to the chief witnesses, who had also been detained to prevent such undue influence. This would be proved by evidence to a jury. The seclusion of the prisoner made sense when one recalled his behaviour when the officer who arrested him let him have a few humane minutes aside with his wife. He gave her cash to aid the killer's flight. He, Erskine, had been authoritatively informed that the tacksman received liberal treatment which included exercise in the open air and such visits from accredited friends and agents as would not impede the enquiry.

There was no basis for the accusation that the prosecutors had conducted a campaign of calumny to discredit the defendant. Who could have led that campaign – Glenure's widow, who knew hardly a soul in Argyll, or her children, who had not yet learned to talk? Yet it had to be admitted that public opinion, inflamed by influential voices, ran strongly hostile to James, but his most powerful enemies were his family, his clan and his notorious behaviour. These were enough to arouse a general belief that he was guilty.

The defence insisted that relations between the factor and his subagent were cordial. This may have been true in the first phase of Glenure's lenient stewardship but James soon abused his position by levying extra charges for the support of Ardsheal's children. The Barons of the Exchequer rightly stepped in and instructed their agent to evict James and anyone who accepted his authority. To the tacksman the decision to eject the five tenants signalled the end of his power. When his efforts to block the warrants failed he resolved that Glenure should die. He recruited Allan Breck, and both men tried to goad potential assassins to the deed. No one volunteered. When Breck came to Aucharn on Monday, 11 May, the plotters determined that he should carry out the atrocity.

Erskine then gave a brief account of the murder which echoed the indictment and Simon Fraser but made two notable additional assertions. First, *several* messengers were sent by James to Fort William to report on Glenure's movements. Second, one of the accused's guns was later discovered bearing marks that showed it had recently been fired. It was impossible that this intimately connected series of incidents could be the result of chance. True, each of Breck's actions was open to an innocent interpretation, but their sequence – the threats, his attempts to engage a killer, the dogging of the victim's footsteps, the change of dress, the flight after the murder – all left no doubt that he was the culprit. By the same reasoning James stood exposed as his accomplice. Each incident in his behaviour, defensible in itself, forged an unbroken chain of proof. He had welcomed to his home Allan, a man who had no personal quarrel with Glenure but who hurried to Aucharn with the news that the factor had returned from Edinburgh; who conferred with, and was clothed by James; who appeared to have used a gun owned by the man in the dock; and who was furnished by him with the necessities for escape.

The contention that James could not be tried before the outlaw had no support in the legal system. The applicable law laid down that there could be no objection to an indictment that charged a person with being an accessory. Charles Robertson, a man who inspired his children and servants to knock down a house, was brought to trial before they were apprehended. That decision won the approval of Sir George Mackenzie. There was no good reason to depart from established practice in the case of the present accused, but for whose assistance the murderer might now be standing before them.

Prestongrange completed the Crown case for 'the relevancy of the libel'. He explained his appearance at a circuit court as the result of a resolution he made on first being shocked at the killing of a King's factor. The assassins were 'guilty not only of a most horrid crime against the laws of God and humanity, but together with this, of a most audacious insult against the most

Caolasnacon and Loch Leven from the heugh of Corrynakiegh

Alan Thomson

Joshua Davidson   In a private Scottish collection

John Campbell, Lord Glenurchy, 3rd Earl of Breadalbane
'. . . he had a creative way with the facts'.

Inverarary Castle

Allan Ramsay   By kind permission of the Scottish National Portrait Gallery

Charles Erskine, Lord Tinwald, Lord Justice-Clerk

gracious and beneficent acts of the King's Government . . .'. He determined to do everything in his power to persuade the dissidents in the Highlands to sub*mit* to the Government which they had several times tried to sub*vert*.

He proposed to limit his address to answering the arguments of the defence. Erskine had started out on the same course but strayed somewhat, and so did the Advocate. He swiftly dismissed the complaint that James had wrongfully been kept in close confinement. Admitting that he was not conversant with the facts, he gave it as his opinion that even if the segregation had lasted longer than it should the accused's defence was not seriously obstructed. James was arrested on 16 May and, if it was true that he had lost a few days' consultation with his advisers, still had plenty of time to prepare his case throughout the succeeding four months.

Of the defence reproach that the private prosecutors engaged all the best lawyers Prestongrange claimed to know the origin. When Glenure's kinsmen had brought him the results of the investigation they were accompanied by three capable advocates. He deliberated with them and it was unanimously decided to put the defendant on trial. All this was quite proper. So the private prosecutors were first to complete their team, but only three counsel were commissioned, leaving many experienced men. The defence had admitted that there was a case to answer and appealed for a trial by jury. He agreed, readily conceding that the opposition should be permitted to bring evidence in support of their client.

Prestongrange dwelt at some length on the question of trying the accessory first. Charles Robertson the demolitionist had been tried under an Act of 1592 which decreed that all persons charged with involvement in a specific crime should be deemed 'art and part' of that crime, and that 'art and part' be understood to mean that all were principals in the offence. Furthermore, in the Robertson case it was successfully pleaded that if the perpetrator were vainly summoned to court he could be declared an outlaw

85

and the trial proceed against his accessory. The trial of James was therefore legal on two counts. The Lord Advocate reminded the court of the wording of the indictment – that the two Stewarts were 'guilty, actors, or art and part' of the crime. Allan Breck was not cited as the principal, nor James as the accessory. It was true that it went on to state that Breck's finger triggered the shot, but the sense of the relevant Act was that both were principals. Suppose, argued Prestongrange, that Allan had died after committing the murder, the defence objection, if upheld, would have freed James of any proceedings, however damning the evidence of his complicity.

At the most recent trial in Edinburgh James More Drummond had been found guilty of hamesucken – assault on a person in his or her own home – forcible marriage, and rape. There was no doubt that he and his accomplices were equally principals in the crime of hamesucken, but his vanished brother Robin was the sole offender on the other charges. The Advocate went on to stress the validity of circumstantial evidence, quoting two celebrated trials in which murderers had been successfully prosecuted on indirect but conclusive testimony. In both cases the guilt of the criminals had been revealed by opportune discoveries. Margaret Stewart and her daughter Elizabeth made sworn statements that when Breck left their home on Tuesday, 12 May he was wearing his French uniform. Sandy Bane exposed this untruth by confessing that he had received the uniform from Margaret's own hands and borne it to Caolasnacon on Saturday, 16 May. 'This discovery was the first thread which the kindred of the deceased got hold of to lead them to a more full detection . . .'

Prestongrange re-stated Erskine's argument that James's actions, regarded collectively, amounted to proof of guilt, though each was capable of an innocuous explanation. He asked judges and assizers to mark well that Allan Breck asked the stockman to take a letter to William, who would give him money. The merchant, a close friend of the accused, was the man to whom he had sent the pedlar for five guineas on the day after the murder. Taken together, those two facts disclosed an agreement reached by the schemers during Allan's stay at Aucharn a few days before Glenure's death. He asked the judges to find that the defence had failed to establish that there was no case to answer.

Thomas Miller, Sheriff-depute of Kirkcudbright, was the final speaker for 'a plea in bar of trial'. After a perfunctory expression of revulsion at the crime he attacked what he described as the intemperate conduct of the dead man's friend in courteous but caustic language. He observed that the prosecutors had admitted that the hand that killed the factor was Allan's. The nature of the murder was such that a single unaided man could have carried it out. Philosophers used the rule of Ockham's Razor, which states that causes should not be multiplied unnecessarily. If one applied this parsimony principle to the present case it was obvious that Breck's sole guilt accounted for all the circumstances of the killing. Much prejudice had been generated against James but he must be presumed innocent until proven guilty, a verdict Miller was confident the evidence would fall short of achieving.

The prosecution alleged that his client contrived the shooting for three reasons – that Glenure had taken the factorship, that he had removed James from his farm, and that he was engaged in extirpating the residents. But Glenure became factor more than three years before his death, and a sequence of letters would be produced to show that his relations with the tacksman throughout most of that period were friendly. That congenial spirit was apparent when Glenure asked James to move out of his farm. He consented without waiting for an official notice. If, therefore, he did not resent his own removal it was unthinkable that the eviction of the others could have fired him to the extent of murder. Such a petty cause could not incense a *wicked* man, let alone one of James's respected character. Nor could Allan Breck's change of clothing implicate his adoptive parent. Proof would be forthcoming that he frequently wore borrowed items for greater security. Would James have lent him his garments, knowing that if he were captured his own role would come into view? Would he let Breck wander the countryside for two days dressed in what was intended to be a disguise? To do so would be to stamp himself as a man who bore no resemblance to the sly conspirator the prosecutors portrayed.

The fact that James communicated with Allan Breck at Caolasnacon was urged as proof that before the murder he knew where his ward would seek refuge. The court had already heard that the defendant received word from Breck via Donald Stewart on the morning after the death. The defence hoped to prove this beyond argument, thus erasing the only particular in the charge that suggested conspiracy. If their Lordships believed there was collusion they would find it hard to explain why someone of James's experience did not provide escape money until after the murder, when contact with Allan could be made only through go-betweens, with greater risk of detection. If he was out of funds on the Monday the plot was allegedly created he could easily have raised a loan before Friday.

The sole other item of consequence was the threats said to have been uttered. Miller regretted that the Lord Advocate had not given any direct quotations or dates and places. Since he had not, the accused could but issue a comprehensive denial, confident that no evidence would emerge to show that he had menaced the life of an innocent gentleman. Counsel finally turned to the question of trying the accomplice before the chief actor, a theme of which his listeners may have felt they had heard enough. He quoted the dog-Latin of statute and textbook to the effect that a man charged with receiving stolen goods should not be judged before the alleged thief. The principal must first be brought to court and if he is found guilty the notional receiver's trial should follow. If the supposed thief is acquitted his partner must be free of any further action. This principle had the support of Sir George Mackenzie, who disapproved of the decision to try Charles Robertson while the men who had razed the house were still at large. In the event of an accessory being tried first the prosecution could not claim to bring sufficient proof of the guilt of the principal, for no Scotsman could be convicted in his absence.

One of the Lord Advocate's arguments for the present order of trial had been that an accessory must not go free if the primary offender escaped or died. That was certainly an inconvenience, but the law was rightly more concerned with protecting the innocent than punishing the criminal, a view enshrined in the adage that it was better that ten guilty men go free than an innocent one suffer. The Advocate's statement that the outlawing of Breck was sufficient grounds for trying James had no footing in law. A proclamation of outlawry was merely a court judgment ordering the seizure of a person's goods for failing to turn up for trial; it held no implication that he was guilty of the offence for which he was summoned. The contention that James and Allan Breck were equally principals derived no authority from the Act he had cited. Its purpose was not to do away with the distinction between principal and accessory: so wrote Sir George Mackenzie and Sir John Skeene. It simply permitted a prosecutor to frame an indictment in broad general terms, the prescribed phrase 'art and part' having the loose meaning of involvement or participation. But if a defendant was unambiguously named as an accessory, as in the current case, he clearly could not be treated as a principal. James More Drummond Macgregor was correctly charged as one, having taken a leading part in the hamesucken and abduction of the widow. He could not have credibly claimed to be an accessory, entitled to be tried after his brother.

Miller concluded the defence case that there was no charge to answer with a brief summing-up of its central proposition. Ancient law, unaffected by the 1592 Act, had fixed the order of partners in crime. Under its terms no judgment could be passed on James until Allan Breck, 'the sole actor in the commission of the murder', was convicted in court. If their Lordships rejected

89

this submission the accused hoped to be allowed to bring evidence to clear him.

The judges refused the plea in bar of trial, granted the defence request to bring vindicatory evidence, and set the time for the start of the jury trial as five o'clock next morning.

6 The Evidence

DARKNESS STILL CLOAKED Inveraray when the judges selected the jury. The panel of assizers, from which relatives of the victim had been scrupulously excluded, comprised forty-five names. Thirty-four hailed from Argyll and eleven from Bute, the two shires forming a single judicial area. Of the four absent assizers three were Argyll men. The residence of the other is not stated. Not one of the Bute assizers was chosen. Their omission may not be as unethical as it sounds, as there is evidence to suggest that it was normal practice to empanel only jurors from the shire where the offence was committed. From the thirty or thirty-one remaining available candidates eleven Campbells were chosen for the fifteen-man jury. Three of them bore the same Christian name as Glenure and one of these was appointed foreman. Another was Campbell of Carwhin, who had witnessed the judicial declarations of most of the central figures in the case, including both of James's. As the right of peremptory challenge to jurors did not then exist the Campbells had a clear and immovable majority. It is said that one or two of the clan refused to serve, pleading their inability to take a detached view, but no names have come down to us. Thus the judges, advised by Stonefield, chose fifteen good men and true, and gave the phrase 'a packed jury' universal currency. Many Scots re-christened it 'a Campbell jury'. Admittedly the practice of hand-picking jurymen had enjoyed a long and dishonourable history before 1752, but seldom before must it have been possible to glance at the names and conclude that the dice were loaded.

Generations of commentators have condemned the composition of the panel that faced James but it has not been without its champions. They have argued that in Inveraray, the hub of Campbell authority, it would have been more unusual than otherwise if the clan had not had majority representation on a jury. Assizer lists were compiled mainly from the ranks of landowners

91

and tacksmen, a large proportion of whom were Campbells. The rent roll for the shire in the year preceding the murder showed that nearly half the landed proprietors were of that name. They formed a recurring majority on each of the few jury trials held at Inveraray at the period, and their preponderance attracted no recorded criticism except in the Glenure case. The insinuation that a panel dominated by Campbells could not be trusted to reach an unbiased verdict has been called harsh in the light of the clan's historical part in replacing the law of the sword with that of the statute. From a practical standpoint it was desirable that the assize roll should include a substantial number of worthies from the town and surrounding area, where the tribe was at its most numerous. Jury service was far from popular, especially among ageing backwoodsmen faced with long journeys on primitive roads. Absenteeism was so rife that heavy fines were imposed to curb it, and to ensure a good attendance Stonefield sensibly drew up lists which included a disproportionate number of local men.

Having empanelled the jury the court proceeded to the evidence. The exhibits for the prosecution consisted of several official documents, the judicial declarations of the Stewart family, sundry letters to and from James, the 'Dear Glen' letter attributed to Allan Oig, the tacksman's two guns, the black jacket confiscated at Aucharn and the clothes worn by Allan Breck and the deceased. The defence exhibits were five letters from Glenure to James. The prosecution presented a list of fifty-one witnesses and their opponents twelve. The two Ballachulishes spoke for both sides, compulsorily for the prosecution, and what little injurious testimony they gave was directed at Allan Breck. The accused, through his lawyers, objected to the inclusion of one witness, Alexander Stewart in Lagnaha, arguing that he had been evicted from Aucharn to make way for James and bore him a grudge. The court overruled the objection. Prestongrange waived his right to call the man, bringing his total of witnesses down to a round fifty. Each testifier's narration was summarised in writing by one of the judges, and cross-examination was permitted at the conclusion of each piece of evidence. Exclusively Gaelic speakers, who made nearly half the total of witnesses, had their contributions turned into English by Stonefield and an assistant interpreter. All the oral evidence was inscribed in the West Circuit Book, which rests in the Scottish Record Office. This phase of the trial ended with the reading of all the documents and writings submitted by both sides.

The story that emerged was understandably more detailed than the one afforded by the extant precognitions. It is probably best assimilated by following the order of events strictly and assuming that every witness told the truth, except in the few cases where someone manifestly lied or was mistaken. In April, 1750, when relations between the factor and his deputy were civil, to put it no higher, Glenure wrote to James conveying his wife's thanks for his good wishes. A year later, by the middle of March, the factor had persuaded him to move out of his farm. Airds offered him the lease of Aucharn and he accepted. He told his new landlord that he did not mind being removed, as he had reason to believe that the surcharges on the land he had just vacated would still go to his brother's children. To his clansman Invernahyle he sounded a different tune. He was surprised and dissatisfied. The factor would never have ousted him if his cousin Ballieveolan had not angled for the property. That land maintained some of the most prolific farms on the estate, whose surplus rents would be lost to Ardsheal's family. He told John Don that he would be willing to drag himself on his knees to a window to take a shot at Glenure. But it was a young herdsman who took up employment with the usurper who felt the full impact of James's anger. The supplanted man berated him for so doing, saying he would get even with him sooner or later, and if he failed during the farm-hand's lifetime he would take it out on his friends after his death. The herdsman had never been employed by James. On 14 March Glenure wrote to James forbidding him to let any part of Ardsheal, Auchindarroch or Aucharn until he had seen him. A letter dated 1 April 1751 and signed 'Allan Stewart' was later found at Aucharn. It stated that

Glenure intended to manage the Ardsheal lands on his own and Ballieveolan planned further infiltration of Glen Duror. But, said the text, it would be 'a Dear Glen' to them before they possessed it. Allan Oig had denied authorship of it and Invernahyle, who was familiar with his writing, was shown it. He said that the hand resembled Allan's but he could not be sure.

One morning around Christmas James was in his brew-house with John More, John Beg and Dugald. They all sampled recently distilled spirits. James told them he was at odds with Glenure over the proportion of tenants' rents to be paid in kind. That man would make himself laird of Appin within five years, he continued, if he carried on at the same rate. James could recall a time when the commoners of the area would never have tolerated Glenure's high-handed ways, and it was the commoners who would suffer from his oppression. He, James, and people like him could always shift for themselves. John Beg remembered discussing those remarks with Dugald, expressing his doubt whether they were a cue to murder or a reproach for disloyalty. Dugald had no recollection of any such duologue. A few days after the brew-house conversation the merry party celebrating Hogmanay at the Kentallen Inn broke up in fistic intoxication. Dugald, who had been sent to the hostelry by Margaret to look after his master, carried the inebriate home with the help of some others. As Dugald told it, James grumbled that if his friends had left him alone he and Glenure would have parted good friends. Why had they not gone home at a respectable hour? They answered that they had stayed to assist him. He accused them of taking Red Colin's side 'to see what they could get by him'. One witness who had lent a hand with the roisterer said he had not heard Glenure's name mentioned, and young Ballachulish, who took part, was not asked the question. Next day Glenure and Ballieveolan went to Aucharn, two-way apologies were proffered and lunch consumed.

In February Allan Breck crossed from France and showed up in Edinburgh. Within days of his advent William met him in the

94

capital and noticed that he was wearing his regimental uniform. He was clothed in the same garb when he called at a friend's house in Rannoch some time in March. At the end of that month he arrived at Aucharn, to find the countryside buzzing with the news of the scheduled evictions. According to James he had a single discussion with his ward about Glenure, but he did not say whether it occurred at this time or later. Allan Breck asked him if he had heard that Serjeant More Cameron, then an exile in France, had come to Appin. He replied that he had not. Allan said that before the serjeant left the Continent he vowed to destroy the factor for his persecution of Lochiel's people. He went on to say that his own intention was to challenge Ballieveolan and his sons to duels for their part in the ejection of James and the tenants. The older man told him they would never fight an inferior, and that if he had crossed the sea to wreak violence he should have stayed where he was. Breck remained for about a week. One morning he took the smaller musket and went out to shoot blackcocks. On his return he complained that the gun had thrice failed to discharge and fired the fourth, missing the target. He visited Callert clad in a black jacket and trousers, and met Charles Stewart the notary. He told him that Colonel Crawfurd was trying to capture him for desertion but that he was in the clear, having surrendered to a justice of the peace after Culloden.

On 3 April James rode off to apply for an injunction, leaving Breck behind. His mission was self-imposed, by the word of three men listed for eviction who testified. They denied having asked him to go. On the same day Allan Breck joined Dugald and John More at the harrow. Their accounts of the ensuing dialogue varied in small points but agreed in essence: Allan told them that he thought little of the common people of Appin for allowing the factor to dispossess them. He was willing and able to arrange a clean escape for anyone who would venture 'to take him out of the way'. In the few days that he tarried in the district Allan set out on a drinking spree with a middle-aged tenant farmer. Uttering repeated maledictions against all Campbells he told a tavern-keeper of the name that if they attempted to evict he would make blackcocks of them. He told the same man that Glenure had reported his presence to Crawfurd, but that he was too cunning for the governor. He had made his peace with the commander-in-chief and now carried his pass in his pocket-book. The landlord asked for a look at it. Allan produced the book, riffled through it, but did not come across a pass. He then tore out a page and said that was it. Time and again he assured the Campbell that he would get even with the factor and, in the words of the landlord's testimony, 'wanted nothing more than to meet him at a convenient place'. A young Stewart who was present swore that he heard the soldier say that he would murder Glenure or Ballieveolan before he left the country. A day or two later, while boozing the hours of darkness away, he promised the pauper something worthwhile if he would fetch him the Red Fox's skin. Towards the end of the first week in April Allan headed back to Rannoch and spent the next three weeks there. While he was away Crawfurd wrote to Airds asking him to look into the gossip that Breck was in the area recruiting for the French service. Airds made some enquiries and reported that the deserter had been in Appin but was now gone.

On the last day of April Allan returned to Aucharn, to which James had ridden back from Edinburgh a few days previously. The tacksman's trip had been eventful. Flushed with drink, he had informed a Campbell that there was nothing he would help him or any of his clan to, except a gallows. The man retorted that James sounded as if he would not mind pulling down their feet, a reference to the practice by which clumsy hangmen of the day finished off their choking clients. Back came the reply that there were some he would not mind treating so, and some he would. He had called Glenure out but the man had declined to fight, he said. Many drams later he assured his travelling companion, Colin Maclaren, that if he was unsuccessful in Edinburgh he would appeal to Parliament, and if he received no satisfaction there he would take the only remaining remedy. On 27 April he reached home again, triumphantly flourishing his piece of paper. On 1 May a deputation headed by Charles the notary served the injunction. While he was at Aucharn the lawyer heard Breck remark that he thought it unfair of Glenure to remove the Ardsheal people and leave the Cameron occupiers undisturbed.

The day after the factor accepted the sist Allan walked several miles to Cuil and stayed the night with friends. He had by then been wearing the black jacket and blue plaid trousers for a month. He told his foster-brother Charles, though possibly not at this time, that James had given him the coat. On that Tuesday he changed into his own outfit and set off on a round of overnight visits, accompanied by Charles. Their first port of call was Appin House, the chief's home, perhaps to pay their respects. On Friday, 8 May the pair reached Fasnacloich, where they spent the weekend at the laird's house, a mile and a half from Glenure's. On Sunday Fasnacloich told Allan that the factor had come home from Edinburgh with an eviction warrant. He responded that if Glenure had a warrant there was nothing more to be said, but if he did not he would not be allowed to eject. Breck also learned, almost certainly from the laird, that Red Colin intended to ride to Maryburgh.

Next morning, Monday, Allan left Fasnacloich. Walking alone, he reached Aucharn in the early afternoon. He saw James, Allan Oig, John More and John Beg in a potato field, resting on the ground. The soldier sat down beside James. The two men held some conversation in English, stated John Beg, who did not speak the language. Allan Oig said they spoke privately for about five minutes. John More noticed no exchange between them, possibly through drowsiness after strenuous labour on a day when there is reason to believe that the weather was warm. After a short time a messenger arrived from Airds asking James to go to Keil to help with the letting of a farm. Walter Stewart the defence counsel said in his opening plea that Allan Breck then walked with his host as far as the house, a distance of fifty yards, where the tacksman left him and took off for Keil. The advocate's assertion was not evidence but it could well have been true. He would assuredly not have made an admission that his client was alone with Breck for a brief period at a crucial time if he had any doubts about its veracity. Neither Allan Oig nor the Maccolls mentioned the two accuseds' stroll to the farmhouse. In fact John More said that Breck remained seated in the field. The balance of evidence seems to be that the co-defendants talked for several minutes.

Not long after Breck reached Aucharn he was followed there by Charles, Fasnacloich's daughter Mary, and Archibald Cameron, her cousin. In the course of the afternoon Breck took off his long French coat and red waistcoat and replaced them with his foster-father's black jacket. He had a talk with Allan Oig, whom he told that Glenure had returned from Edinburgh and was bent on executing the eviction notices. He entered a field where John More and John Beg were covering potatoes and lent a hand. After a while they were joined by Donald Macdonald, a brother of Glencoe. He too bore the latest tidings. In the ensuing discussion Allan said that 'devil a bit of the new tenants would get possession unless they had a warrand to show, or come in by force.'

James came back from Keil before nightfall. To Allan Oig he seemed sober, but that was not the man's own recollection. He said that when he had finished his task Airds gave him and some others three or four bottles of whisky. James lowered his share and swayed home 'concerned with drink'. He could not quite remember whether he supped with the soldier. He did, together with his family, Mary Stewart and Cameron. By James's account the news that Glenure was to go to Maryburgh before returning to effect the evictions was broken to him by either Allan Breck, Charles or Mary; he could not remember which. The large group encircled the table for supper, during which James and his ward had no private converse that Cameron could observe. After the meal the young men went out to the barn, where

Breck shared a bed with Charles, and Allan Oig another with Cameron.

At dawn James set off for Appin House to do some business for Airds. Allan Breck rose later. Before departing he asked Margaret 'if she had any commands for Rannoch'. He left the house in the company of Charles, telling him he was bound for Glencoe. He was wearing a blue bonnet and dun greatcoat over a black jacket and blue plaid trousers. They walked to Kentallen and parted there. Breck strode off towards Ballachulish House, just over three miles distant, where he met young Fasnacloich, who remarked on his change of dress. He said he did it because the day was warm. Someone mentioned that Glenure had left for Maryburgh and Allan asked some questions about it. In the afternoon the two visitors went off to pay a call on Isobel Macdonald at Carnoch, now part of the modern village of Glencoe. Breck was only a short time there before crossing Loch Leven and spending the night at Helen Cameron's house in Callert. Next day, Wednesday, he made a brief return to Carnoch, staying for about a quarter of an hour, before walking to Ballachulish, where the ferryman saw him near the south landing-stage in the evening. That night he lodged with the laird. On the following morning, Glenure's last, Allan went fishing in the stream above the house shortly before midday. At some time after noon he turned up at the ferry, drew the boatman's attention, gestured him aside and asked if the factor had passed across. On being told that he had not he walked off towards the road which Glenure was later to travel.

Two days previously James had come back from Appin House in the afternoon to find that Allan Breck had departed some hours earlier. Believing that Charles Stewart the notary was away from home he decided to contact the man's father, Alexander, another lawyer. He sent John Beg with a letter urging him to come to Aucharn and act for him in the matter of the evictions. The little messenger took a roundabout route and did not attain his destination until Wednesday morning. Alexander had gone fishing and did not read the letter until that night. His reply, refusing the assignment because of fatigue, reached Aucharn early on Thursday morning. By that time the word had spread throughout Appin that the factor would dine at the Kentallen Inn that evening. James had also heard that the younger Stewart notary was at home. He sent John Beg with a letter to him, impressing on his servant the need for all possible speed. He told him that its purpose was to summon the lawyer to Appin to scan Glenure's eviction documents for flaws. John Beg was further instructed to call at William's shop and collect money for cattle James had bought for him. If William did not send the money the tacksman would not deliver the cows.

John Beg hurried to Kentallen, whence he was rowed across Loch Linnhe by the landlord and John More. A few miles from Maryburgh he met Glenure, his servant Mackenzie and Mungo, all mounted. Glenure hailed the messenger and asked him where he had come from. John Beg told him, then exchanged a word or two with Mackenzie, whom he knew. He hurried on towards Maryburgh and entered the village about noon. He called at William's shop and told him of his errand. The merchant said that the notary was out of town. He opened the letter and read: 'Dear Charles, Not knowing of your Return from Muidart sent for your father Tuesday afternoon But the Rascall I sent went not by Glencrearan that night by which he missed the old man who went a fishing as you'l see by the Inclosed early that morning wch I reckon a very great misfortune, The next and best I can think of is that you be here without fail this night if you should hyre a horse as every thing must go wrong without a Person can act and that I can trust. This is such a Tye upon all the members of our family that I will press you no further but do depend on seeing you once this night and I am DC your own &c Sic Subr. James Stewart Aucharn May 14th 8 oClock morning 1752 P.S. As I have not time to write to William let him send down immediately £8 sterling to pay 4 milk Cows I bought for his use at Ardsheal.'

William said that if Charles the notary decided to go he would take a boat. In any case Glenure had a lawyer in tow who could act for James. As for the cattle, he had sent a letter to John Beg's master about the matter that morning. William did not hand over any money. With what seems to have been characteristic vagueness he could not later recall whether he told the emissary that he was low in funds. Rushing away, John Beg took a short cut and came to North Ballachulish around four o'clock. He found Glenure engaged in a dispute with a group of locals about the employment of a ferryman. Noticing John Beg, the factor voiced surprise that the tireless trekker had caught up with him. 'Sir, you travel better than I do,' he said. 'I am in a haste,' was the reply. John Beg asked the ferryman to take him over at once and the man, after some demur, did his bidding. On the south side the messenger soon met old Ballachulish. He told the laird of James's quest for a lawyer and Ballachulish asked him to tell the tacksman that he would make himself available next morning to inspect Glenure's warrant. John Beg hurried off, then veered left onto the gently rising bridle-path. He neither met nor saw anyone there.

About half an hour after John Beg crossed the narrows Red Colin and his party followed. They had been joined at the ferry by Donald Kennedy, the sheriff's deputy. Shortly they met old Ballachulish. The factor dismounted and the two lairds walked together perhaps half a mile to where the woodland path began to climb. Ballachulish took his leave of Glenure, who remounted. When he came up to Mungo the young man asked if the Stewart had said anything about the evictions. Glenure said he had not. They reached a stretch where the track narrowed, making it difficult to ride two abreast. Mungo moved ahead and was about forty yards from his uncle when the shot rang out. He dismounted, ran back, then probably helped Glenure to the ground before taking a few paces up the slope. He saw 'a man, with a short dark-coloured coat, and a gun in his hand, going away from him; and, as the deponent came nearer him, he mended his pace, and disappeared by high ground interjected betwixt him and the deponent; and he was at so great a distance, that the deponent thinks he could not have known him, tho' he had seen his face.' This direct quotation from Mungo's evidence is totally at variance with his precognition, when he 'observed a man with a gun in his hand cloathed as he thinks in a short dun cullour'd coat & breeches of the same . . .'. Mungo ordered Mackenzie to gallop to Kentallen and fetch Ballieveolan. He did so, but the man was not there. He rode on to Aucharn, reported the murder and asked James if he knew Ballieveolan's whereabouts. On hearing of Glenure's death the tacksman cried: 'Lord bless me, was he shot?' He wrung his hands and hoped aloud that no innocent people might be blamed. Margaret dissuaded him from attending the corpse for fear of the dead man's friends but he enjoined his neighbours to do so.

To hide the weapons was now essential. John Beg swore that Dugald told him that Margaret had given the order to conceal the arms. Dugald said that Allan Oig commanded John Beg and himself to take the larger gun from the brew-house and put it out of sight. The clash of testimony can be blamelessly set down to the confused and frantic disorder that must have reigned in what Stevenson aptly named The House of Fear. Both labourers agreed that they hid four swords and the larger gun in the thatch of the outhouses. Both testified that Allan Oig told them he had already hidden the smaller gun under the girnel, or granary-chest, in the barn. He assured Dugald that it would be undetected. The musket normally stood in the barn, which could be locked. At that time of year, however, it was unlocked, as there were no crops in the girnel. John Beg had seen the weapon on one of the two days preceding the murder; he was not sure which. He could not speak for the day itself, having gone to Maryburgh.

Ballachulish's servant-girl said that she had occasion to leave the house as night was falling. She spied the figure of Allan Breck at a goat-house a little farther up the brae. He asked her what was the cause of the commotion in the houses. She told him. He inquired 'who could have committed the murder' and she replied that she did not know. He requested her to tell Donald Stewart, who lived at Ballachulish House, to go to James and ask him to send some money. She delivered the message to Donald, probably very shortly after the encounter. His version was that she entered the house and told him that someone wanted to speak to him. When he left the room she said that it was Breck, and indicated where to find him. Donald confronted the skulker and accused him of the murder, which he denied. Donald said he did not believe him. Breck declared that he was going to Caolasnacon and appealed to him to ask James to send cash there. The accounts of these two witnesses differed in the critical detail of whether the girl delivered a short, specific message from Breck, who said nothing of fleeing to Caolasnacon, or whether she told Donald that the fugitive wished to see him. If the maid spoke the truth James was to receive a plea to send money to an unnamed spot – unnamed, it must have occurred to some jurymen, because prearranged. If Donald's story was factual it was he who told James where to despatch the cash. His evidence was therefore the defendant's lifeline, in a more than figurative sense.

In the small hours of the next day Allan knocked at Glencoe's window in Carnoch. The Macdonald chief came out with his stepmother Isobel. The visitor broke the news of Glenure's death and said he was leaving the country. They asked him no questions about the assassination but invited him inside. He declined and went off.

Later that Friday morning James had two conversations whose order of occurrence was as crucial as their content. One was with Donald Stewart, who went to Glen Duror and spoke with him near his house at about ten o'clock. Donald reported his twilight meeting with Breck and the fugitive's request to send the necessaries to him at Caolasnacon. The other talk was with Sandy Bane, whom James directed to go to William and ask for cash for Allan's escape. The merchant and his wife attested that Sandy entered their shop no later than noon. If they were right the pedlar must have started his sixteen-mile walk before Donald spoke to James. And if that was the case James must have known Breck's whereabouts and needs *before* Donald brought the message. Sandy Bane said that he set out about noon and reached Maryburgh early in the evening. If he was correct the defence story of the sequence obviously held together: James received a cry for help and quickly responded.

Sandy, by his own oath, was instructed to make an urgent demand for five pounds or guineas for Breck and four pounds to pay for cattle. The money must be sent, even if it had to be borrowed from twenty purses. William must also give John Don Maccoll five pounds if he should come to ask for it. This latter request had found no mention in Sandy's precognitions or the indictment, nor had any of the prosecution lawyers referred to it during the debate on the relevancy of the libel. If true, it meant that James attempted to set up a cash credit for John Don on the Friday. Next day Allan asked the stockman to take a begging letter to William. The message carried by Donald had said nothing of either John Don or a money credit, which strongly suggested that the arrangement had been fixed in advance. James had a further requirement of William. Would he let Cameron of Glen Nevis know that the horse James had bought for him was ready for collection? As Sandy told it, he asked the shopkeeper for both cash and credit and received the same reply as had John Beg on the previous day: he was out of money. William persuaded him to go to Glen Nevis with the news about the horse and spend the night there. He promised to give him the funds next day on his return journey through Maryburgh. On the morrow Sandy walked back and met William in the street. The merchant went into his house and his wife soon came to the door and gave Sandy three guineas.

The stories told by William and his wife differed on some points with the hawker's, and indeed in a few with each other's. They said that when Sandy entered their shop he asked for five pounds for the cows. William said he could not spare that amount. His wife intervened to propose that Sandy go to Glen Nevis and come back next day. He did so and met her in the street, where she took three guineas from her purse and gave them to him. Two facts emerged clearly from the three testimonies: Sandy spoke to William at least once, and possibly twice, and he had two conversations with his spouse. Neither William nor his wife said that their caller mentioned a cash accommodation for John Don.

In the early afternoon after Sandy Bane had set out for Maryburgh the younger Ballachulish turned up at Aucharn. James told him that Donald had relayed an appeal from Allan Breck, and that he intended to send him money. Ballachulish could not recall whether his tutor told him where he had been directed to deliver the cash. At about four o'clock in the afternoon John Beg and Dugald were ordered by their master and mistress to remove the weapons from the thatch and hide them up the brae. John Beg recovered the smaller musket from under the girnel where Allan Oig had said he hid it. The gun was unloaded. The labourers took all the arms up the hillside, overtaking Katharine the dairymaid on the way. She was carrying a sack containing, she told them, Breck's French garments. All the articles were concealed on the brae. The squad captain who uncovered the little musket gave evidence that he put his finger down the muzzle and it came out black. He formed the impression that it had recently been fired. He was asked in cross-examination whether a gun which had been stored for a month in a dirty place might not also blacken the finger. His frigid reply was that he could not say, being unused to seeing weapons treated in that way.

On the next afternoon, Saturday, 16 May, Allan Breck drew John Don's attention by whistling from the heugh of Corrynakiegh. The stockman accused him of the murder. Allan replied by asking what he had heard about it. That two men were sighted fleeing the wood of Lettermore, said John Don, one of whom was the soldier himself. Allan denied being the killer, adding that he had heard that one man was seen. He realised that he would be suspected, but was less worried by any evidence that might be brought against him, if captured, than by a charge of desertion, and he was afraid that 'Allan Stewart the pannel's son's tongue was not so good as his father's . . .'. John Don begged him to clear off lest he bring trouble on him and his family. His answer was that he would remain in the neighbourhood for eight days 'unless some necessaries he expected came to him', and that if the money had not arrived by the following morning John Don would have to take a letter to William. Taking a powder-horn from his pocket he watered its contents to make ink. He wrote a letter, but the bouman at first refused to deliver it in case he was caught. 'If captured, you must swallow it,' Breck ordered the jittery grazier. John Don promised that if he should decide to go to Maryburgh next day he 'might possibly' carry the letter. Allan asked him to fetch a peck of meal from Callert or Carnoch, a request which was turned down flat. When the two men parted they arranged to meet next day.

Some hours later Sandy Bane got back to Aucharn after his partially successful fund-raising mission to Maryburgh. Very soon word came that James had been arrested at Inshaig. Sandy and Margaret rushed there, and the apprehending officer allowed his prisoner a few private words with his wife and friend. James extracted two guineas from a purse and gave them to Margaret. He asked Sandy to take them, together with the three guineas he had received from William, to Breck. The pedlar could not remember whether he said anything about the clothes. The military set off for Fort William with James, Allan Oig and John Beg. Margaret sent Katharine to fetch the French garb from the hillside. The girl revealed that another servant later told her that her mistress wanted her to say nothing of what she knew about the clothes. Sandy asked Margaret where he would find Allan Breck. At Caolasnacon, was the reply, but if he did not meet him there he was to leave his burden with John Don.

After nightfall the reluctant courier started out on the ten-mile march. As he was scared of travelling alone in the dark he took his sister along for most of the way. On reaching the grazing farm early on Sunday morning he hid the clothes at the root of a fir tree and made for the stockman's house. On the way he met the man himself. He asked him if he had seen Allan Breck, and John Don said he had not. Sandy declared himself surprised, as he had been sent to bring him money and clothes. The other then admitted that he had met the soldier on the previous afternoon and he was now lying doggo in the heugh. Sandy reported that James and Allan Oig had been arrested and that Allan Breck was thought to have shouldered the gun. He handed over the five guineas and pointed out the spot where he had concealed the uniform. John Don warned him to keep his mouth shut about delivering the needful; as an unsupported witness Sandy could not prove that he had done so. He further directed the messenger's attention to the fact that he could honestly swear he had not given him the clothes, since he had merely indicated where they lay. He asked Sandy to beg a peck of meal for the fugitive from Callert or Carnoch but the weary wayfarer would have none of it. The pair went to John Don's house and Sandy snatched a few hours' sleep. After a meal the refreshed traveller turned his steps towards Glen Duror, where he made a report to Margaret, who looked pleased at the upshot.

That night Allan Breck knocked at the stockman's window with such force that the shutter fell in. The householder rose from his bed and went out in his nightshirt. He told the visitor that his cousin Sandy had brought the cash and clothing. Then he took the garments from the foot of the tree and gave them to Allan, together with the money. He told him that James and Allan Oig had been taken up. His response was that he had expected it, but it did not matter much as there could be no proof against them. He 'expressed some apprehension lest Allan Stewart, son to the pannel, might be betrayed by his own tongue.' John Don suggested that his caller take himself off, now that he had acquired what he wanted. Allan said he would depart next morning when he had returned the apparel he was then wearing. The stockman must restore it to Margaret. Breck did not keep the appointment but left the clothes outside the door. In a jacket pocket John Don found the powder-horn. The faintly engraved design on its flat surface and the crack sealed with red wax made it a distinctly recognisable artefact.

On that Monday Allan Breck, clothed in his uniform under a dun greatcoat, called at the Rannoch home of an uncle. There he remained for a couple of days. His uncle exhorted him to make a clean breast of all he knew about the murder and he swore an oath that he had never seen Glenure, alive or dead. So persistently did his host urge him to unburden himself that Breck flew off the handle and the uncle dropped the subject. The soldier resumed his flight and reached Innerhadden at the east end of Loch Rannoch towards the end of May. He asked the landlord of an inn for food and was given bread and cheese. The landlord noticed a holster under his left arm. This was the last publicly admitted glimpse of Allan Breck in Scotland.

One day during his captivity in the fort James sent for a barber to shave him. He confided that he feared nothing but that his servants might be bribed to turn against him. He asked the barber to tell John Beg and Dugald 'to say nothing but truth, to keep their minds to themselves, and he would take care of them'. He gave the man a shilling and promised him more next time. The barber then shaved Allan Oig, whom he told of his father's message to the servants. Allan gave him half a crown and the barber delivered James's admonition to the Maccolls.

On the evidence summarised above, the jury were to pronounce on whether James should hang. A dramatic incident in the course of this phase of the trial may have swayed their judgment. After Campbell of Airds had given his testimony Miller rose to cross-examine him on the defendant's good character. Argyll forbade it on the grounds that it was an irregular procedure that would leave the accused open to rebutting evidence. Miller insisted that he was entitled to elicit that his client was a God-fearing man who was usually engaged in looking after widows and orphans. The duke asked what kind of character the defendant had displayed in the 'Forty-five. The advocate admitted that James had been a junior officer in the rebel forces, but as he had been pardoned the defence had the right, never before refused, to bear out his good name. Argyll asked how he could hope to prove the good character of a man who had been guilty of rebellion, a crime that embraced most other crimes, such as treason, murder, rapine, oppression and perjury. He developed his theme for nearly half an hour, condemning the barbarity of semi-civilised Highlanders. He refused further questioning of Airds. *By-stander* wrote that James then turned to Edinglassie and said, 'It is all over now; my lawyers need give themselves no further trouble about me: my doom is as certain as if it were pronounced. I always dreaded this place, and the influence that prevails in it: but this outdoes all. God forgive him.' Lord Milton, a former Lord Justice-Clerk and confidant of the duke, considered his discourse an uplifting sermon for the packed church.

The loss of Airds as a character witness was a sharp setback for the defence. At forty-seven Donald Campbell epitomised the experience and competence that had raised his clan to greatness and were indispensable to the conduct of public business. He had served without pay as a captain in the Argyll militia in the Rising. His commanding officer entrusted him with the task of keeping a war diary, and he was present at Culloden. He wrote a report on the engagement that earned his general's comment: 'Airds's account of the battle is very distinct. He's a very pretty fellow in every shape.' His peace-time responsibilities grew. At the time of the trial he was a justice of the peace, Crown factor for Morvern and a member of the Commissioners of Supply for Argyll. Loyal Hanoverian though he was, he showed his breadth of mind by employing a Stewart as subagent. He was a frequent guest at Inveraray Castle, where he was to dine years later with Boswell. That he would have spoken well of James can hardly be called in question. It was he who made Aucharn available to the tacksman when Glenure compelled him to leave his previous holding. James's expertise in the letting of property was valued and utilised by the Campbell, as the events of the Monday before the murder make clear. Airds showed his gratitude to his adviser by leasing him part of the farm, a concession that may have raised frowns among other factors, who had been forbidden to let lands to forfeited persons' kinsmen. In his capacity as justice of the peace Airds was present at, and witnessed with his signature, the declarations of James. He observed from close range his tenant's reactions to searching questions. What he saw and heard did not deter him from offering to go bail for him. When James 'papered' Allan Breck he said that Airds and Appin would stand bail for any amount, a guarantee he could have given only if Airds had assented. A clue to the Campbell's willingness to speak up for James may be found in a quotation from *By-stander*. Of Mungo's evidence about the running gunman he wrote: 'There is something incredible in Mungo's story; which, in several circumstances, differs greatly from the way he told it to Airds, Appin, and others, the day after the murder was committed.'

7 Closing Speeches

BETWEEN FIVE AND six o'clock on Sunday morning the last witness spoke his last word and the judicial declarations were read aloud. The court had listened to the evidence without an adjournment for a scarcely credible period of forty-eight hours. How it coped with the problems posed by hundreds of spectators, officials and witnesses can hardly be imagined. The weather, unseasonably warm and dry, must have rendered the daylight hours oppressive and drawn yearning glances from somnolent and sweltering jurors to the blue skies beckoning through the windows. Prestongrange privately decided that the strain of such trials on officers of the court, especially the advocates and jurymen, was excessive, and wondered if the law should be changed.

He rose to address the jury in the closing submission for the Crown. Leading off with an expression of regret that they had been obliged to endure the most protracted circuit trial held in Argyll, the Advocate delivered a speech that must have lasted for well over an hour. He lamented the spirit of barbarism that still lingered in the Highlands, as exhibited in James More's kidnap of the widow. Like the present defendant, the Macgregor had not been motivated by personal gain; his crime was carried out to benefit his outlaw brother, the tacksman's to exact revenge for being deprived of the surcharges with which he supported his brother's children. Prestongrange recounted in detail the management of the Ardsheal estate between 1746 and Glenure's move to eject the tenants. He emphasised that it was James who let the holdings to those tenants during his unofficial factorship before Glenure was appointed. Artfully he made capital out of James's objection to Alexander Stewart in Lagnaha's testifying for the prosecution. That objection, he contended, sprang from the tacksman's certainty that Alexander was embittered against him by being removed from Aucharn to make way for him. It

111

showed just how deeply the defendant resented his own extir-pation. Further proof of James's fury was proffered by the herdsman he had menaced for going to work for Ballieveolan.

Turning to the accused's threats to Glenure, Prestongrange quoted at length from the summarised evidence of no fewer than seven witnesses. He ended with James's declaration to Colin Maclaren that he would take his case all the way up to Parliament and, if that failed him, he would adopt the only other course open to him. No other *legal* course was open to him, stressed the Advocate. He then dwelt on the testimony of eight people who heard Breck breathe homicidal intentions. It was significant that both threateners expressed indignation at the same stroke of policy, the removal of James and the tenants. By the defendant's own word Breck said he would fight Ballieveolan for occupying James's farm. The outlaw was further envenomed by the mistaken belief that Glenure had informed on him to Colonel Crawfurd.

The details of the plot were settled on the evening of the Monday preceding the murder. A few minutes sufficed, because the decision had long since been taken. Allan was to commit the deed, flee to Caolasnacon and wait for James to send money or have it conveyed by William. On Thursday the defendant sent John Beg with the letter whose postscript demanded of William eight pounds for the cattle. The fact that he had not yet delivered them showed how badly he needed cash on the very day Glenure met his end. He had not since offered any explanation of why he needed it. A few hours before the ambush Allan turned up at the ferry to find out if the factor had crossed. He was not carrying the fishing-rod he had taken from Ballachulish House. Before the afternoon was out Breck – if he really was the killer – had achieved his stated desire to meet Glenure 'at a convenient place'. The wood was in all surety convenient both for the commission of the act and unobserved flight to a nearby place of refuge. James responded to the dreadful news by saying 'Lord bless me, was he shot?'. He voiced his fear that it would bring trouble to the district. Clearly he had himself in mind. That evening, when the weapons were hidden, no one saw the shorter gun which Allan Oig claimed he stowed under the granary-box. Ballachulish's servant-maid gave evidence that on the same evening she met Allan Breck above the house. He gave her a message for Donald but did not ask to speak to him. Donald swore that she told him Allan wished to see him. Some hours later the fugitive woke Isobel Macdonald and Glencoe and broke the news of the slaying. Neither asked any questions about it: there was no need.

When Donald delivered the message next morning James directed suspicion at Serjeant More Cameron in a blatant effort to divert attention from his friend. He sent Sandy Bane to Maryburgh for cash and to arrange a credit for John Don Maccoll. The pedlar stated that this happened around noon, but William and his wife said that he arrived at their shop no later than noon. Assuming that they were right, Sandy must have set out long before James was told by Donald that Breck had gone to Caolasnacon. Throughout their conversation in his shop William did not question Sandy about the murder or ask who was suspected: inquiries were superfluous. On the same afternoon, when the weapons were re-sited, the smaller gun was found to be unloaded. At the same time Katharine the dairymaid hid Allan Breck's clothes, and Margaret later warned her to say nothing about the incident if she was questioned.

Prestongrange directed the jury's attention to the importance of John Don's contribution and the totally convincing manner in which it was expressed. Quoting extensively from the text he reminded the jury of the stockman's face-to-face accusation, Allan Breck's virtual imputation of guilt to James and Allan Oig, the powder-horn and the letter to the merchant. John Don was one of only three men to look Allan Breck in the eye and call him murderer, the others being Donald Stewart and his own uncle. In Appin, Breck's was the solitary name advanced as a suspect, said the ferryman. The alehouse-keeper who was the last witness to see him declared that reports of his guilt preceded him to Rannoch. Old Ballachulish formed the conclusion that Allan was the culprit when he did not return to his house on the tragic day.

The transaction with the barber in Fort William was well worth consideration. James told the man he feared nothing but that his servants would be bribed to turn against him, and asked him to take a verbal message to the two Maccolls in their separate cells. They were to speak only the truth, keep their minds to themselves, and he would take care of them.

No doubt the jury were dismayed by the falsehoods in the declarations of Margaret and her daughter. Their story that Breck left Aucharn dressed in his regimental coat had been demolished by a 'cloud of witnesses'. Margaret's own servants and Sandy Bane proved that the clothes were hidden by Katharine and later carried to Caolasnacon.

The Lord Advocate conceded that he was duty bound to prove that Allan Breck fired the shot. He reviewed the outlaw's actions from the weekend before the murder until he was lost to sight in Rannoch. They left no room for doubt that he was the killer. The immediate concern of the jury must be the degree of the co-defendant's complicity. When the investigators discovered that the pedlar delivered the cash and Allan wrote a letter drawing on the credit James was deep in trouble. He perceived that it was vital to show that he had received a plea for cash from Breck which disclosed where to send it. Ballachulish's maid was induced to tell the tale of the meeting on the brae at dusk, and Donald swear that he carried the message. Their stories were mutually contradictory. It should be noted that those two witnesses were connected with the Ballachulish family, all of whom were committed to the cause of the accused. The laird's son disregarded a summons to assizer service in order to act as a witness at James's proposed protest. In August he went to Edinburgh and sat in on discussions while the defence lawyers prepared their case. Those facts should be borne in mind before accepting the word of any

114

of that family concerning conversations they had held with James when no third party was present.

Even if it were granted that James's concocted tale of the message was true it would still fail to explain why Breck wrote to William. He had not heard from his foster-father that he had set about furnishing the credit. How then did Breck, out of contact with James in his leafy retreat, know he must send the letter? What really happened was that James coached witnesses to say that the fugitive sent him an appeal but he forgot to provide a witness that he had sent a return message to Allan telling him how to get his hands on the money.

The other arguments for the defence scarcely deserved a reply. That it had been shown that 12 May was not the first date on which Allan Breck wore James's clothes did not alter the fact that they were more suitable for an ambuscade than his own. The tacksman's efforts to procure a lawyer on the fatal day were designed to line up a last-ditch fight against the evictions in case the plot should miscarry. The letter papering Breck was a transparent bluff unmasked by the defence's own admission that James financed his escape. In addition to the other proofs of guilt there was compelling evidence that the crime was committed with the shorter musket belonging to the defendant. All these facts must be taken into account in reaching a verdict. 'In all circumstantial evidence there is a possibility of innocence, even without supposing any of the witnesses perjured.' If the jury were to conclude that Allan Breck alone was guilty they must acquit James, but if they decided otherwise it was their duty to convict.

The final speech of the trial was made for the defence by George Brown, sheriff of Forfar. He led off by re-listing the handicaps his client had suffered, warning the jurors against passion or prejudice. It was incumbent on the opposition to prove not only that Allan Breck did the deed but that his guardian previously conspired with him. The Lord Advocate had admitted that there was no direct evidence of either of those charges. The

115

circumstantial testimony on which he had based his case must be conclusive, and if that testimony could be shown to have an explanation favourable to the accused it must be judged to have failed. Brown then gave a summary of the events leading up to the week of the murder, dwelling on James's good name, his friendship with Red Colin, and the factor's written acknowledgment that James collected surcharges for Ardsheal's family. Twice during the week in which Glenure died the defendant took steps to summon a lawyer.

The jury must be careful to draw a distinction between the evidence against each of the accused. In the indictment and the Lord Advocate's closing address it was inseparably mingled. The allegation that Allan was told that Glenure would return on Thursday via the Ballachulish ferry received no support. All he knew was that the factor had set out for Lochaber. Breck donned the black coat and blue trousers to lend a hand with the potatoes, not for the purpose of disguise.

The prosecution said that Allan loitered near the ferry, awaiting Glenure. The truth was that he did not know whether the man would journey that way. If he had known, he assuredly would not have gone to Carnoch and Callert, both places miles from the factor's return route. His most compromising act was to take flight on the day of the crime, which he later justified to several people as essential for a deserter, while vigorously protesting his innocence. As for the only other source of suspicion against him, namely his minatory utterances, the chief prosecutor himself seemed to allow that they were not enough to condemn him.

Whether or not the jury believed Breck guilty, there was no worthwhile evidence that James was implicated. His unsullied reputation alone was sufficient answer to the charge of this most unnatural crime. Moreover he was too astute to think he could gain anything by it, knowing that Glenure would be replaced forthwith and official eyes turn to him straight away. It was inconceivable that his client could have planned an act that promised nothing but ruin for himself and his family. His

116

letter to Charles the notary, written on the day the factor died, proved that he was determined on a course within the law. That letter had been produced by the *prosecution*, a fact which added to its substance. James told the bearer, John Beg, that its purpose was to invite Charles to Aucharn to scrutinise the warrant next morning. In it the tacksman begged him to come that night 'without fail'. He furthermore recruited responsible observers for his protest. It was at his earnest entreaty that young Ballachulish refused to go to Inveraray in order to be present, as they had heard him attest.

The three reasons given in the indictment for James's animosity towards Glenure were his acceptance of the factorship, his removal of the accused from his farm, and the proposed evictions. The first was refuted by the factor's friendly letters and his appointment of James as deputy agent. The departure from the farm was amicably agreed without resort to law, as a reliable witness had confirmed. As for the evictions, it was beyond understanding that so minor a cause could trigger so savage an effect, particularly as the accused was unrelated to any of the tenants.

Much had been made of 'certain foolish expressions' of a menacing nature spoken by the defendant. The jury well knew that men often swore hollow resolutions of mayhem. Evidence of such outbursts was always dubious, relying as it did on proverbially inaccurate recall of bygone conversations. The omission in the indictment of any details of those threats robbed the defence of any chance to disprove them. If, when drawing up the charges, the Advocate had precise information of the incidents it was his duty to include it, but if not, he should have left out the allegations. John Don's story that James told him he would shoot Glenure beggared belief. At the period when his client was said to have made the remark the two men were on demonstrably good terms. Of the other blustering expressions he would only say that some could be given a harmless interpretation and others were provoked by drink.

The indictment asserted that the plot was devised on the Monday afternoon. Not only was there no evidence that the defendants had discussed it that day but *Crown* witnesses had proved as conclusively as the facts allowed that they could not possibly have done so. John More deposed that he observed no private communication between the men. John Beg said they had a brief chat in English. Dugald, Katharine, Archibald Cameron and Airds all gave testimony, the sum of which was that the co-accused were never alone together long enough to draft a scheme. This obviously undermined the foundations of the opposing case.

No human could believe that the defendant gave Allan his own clothes before sending him to commit murder. While they might help to disguise the assassin they were sure to incriminate the accomplice. There was no evidence that James gave Breck the garments. It *had* been proved that the soldier changed into clothes belonging to his host or Allan Oig, but 'it would be ridiculous to say that a party could be convicted as an accessory to a murder because that the murderer had on his clothes at the time when the crime was committed.' Allan Breck had worn that attire on other occasions, so the fact that he was dressed in it on the murder day could not be used against James.

Brown then broached the theme of John Beg's alleged spying mission, but he had hardly begun when he was noisily interrupted. A Campbell juryman cried out: 'Pray sir, cut short; we have enough of it, and are quite tired, the trial having lasted long.' An angry hubbub rose from his colleagues. Some spectators thought they were remonstrating with the heckler, others that they were backing his protest. This interjection when a man's life was in peril, while it cannot be excused, can be partially understood. For fifty hours a blizzard of words had swirled over the jury, and they were now undergoing their eighth address in three days. It is little wonder that one of the exhausted hearers was pushed beyond the limits of tolerance when every argument had been expounded, rebuffed and reiterated. When order was restored the advocate reminded his audience that the innkeeper at Kentallen had sworn that the whole district was alert to the news that Glenure was due at his house that evening. Why then should John Beg have found it necessary to cross into Lochaber to track the victim when he could have simply awaited his arrival at the ferry? And why, when the little servant met the factor's party on their way south, did he then continue to Maryburgh if his task was to report their position?

The trivial charge that when Mackenzie sobbed out the news of the murder James displayed no sign of surprise or distress was contradicted by the oath of the messenger himself. The accused's failure to attend the corpse had been convincingly explained as due to fear of attack by armed kinsmen of Glenure.

If James knew when he sent the money that Breck was the murderer it would have been a punishable offence, though understandable in the light of their relationship, but his client denied knowing any such thing. All he had been told was that Allan had proclaimed his innocence and was in want of necessities to get him to a ship. He responded in the manner of any other good-natured man.

The Lord Advocate had attempted to show that the despatch of cash must have been previously concerted, since James knew where to send it. But the testimony of Ballachulish's maid and Donald Stewart established the link. A witness swore he saw Donald and James converse on the Friday morning. The young Ballachulish told of his meeting with the tacksman that afternoon, when James reported his talk with Donald. The public prosecutor had made much of the fact that the two vital witnesses, Donald and the maid, were connected with the Ballachulish family, that in some parts of their evidence they were unsupported, and there were discrepancies between their versions of the message to Donald from Allan Breck. To take the first point, the laird of Ballachulish was unrelated to the accused, and if he had testified for the defence there could have been no valid objection. Hence his son-in-law and his servant-girl should not be charged with bias in favour of James. (Brown seems to have blundered badly here: Ballachulish *did* speak for the defence. It is possible, though very unlikely, that the printer misread his script.) As to their being single witnesses, the prosecutor should note how much of his own evidence was unsupported and explain why John Don and the pedlar should be believed and the defendant's witnesses discredited. It was true that Donald and the girl differed about the exact wording of Breck's message, but such trifles should be ignored. Indeed, if their stories had precisely tallied there would have been just as much cause for misgivings, if not more.

It seemed most likely that William and his wife mistook the time that Sandy Bane entered their shop. The pedlar sounded more sure of his facts, declaring that he left Aucharn at noon and reached Maryburgh in the early evening. This accorded with Donald's assertion that he spoke to James at ten o'clock that morning. How strange that the Lord Advocate should believe those parts of Sandy's story that buttressed his cause and rejected those that did not.

Much of the prosecution case was based on the stockman's romantic tale of Breck's writing a letter and pressing him to take it to William. Coupled with Sandy Bane's evidence that James asked for a cash credit, it was advanced as unassailable proof that the accused men had reached prior agreement on how the money should be paid. But John Don's fiction, being uncorroborated, should not be regarded as legally acceptable. Equally open to mistrust was Sandy's story. The indictment, when outlining his actions in an account that could have come only from his own lips, made no reference to a cash credit. That allegation emerged after the charges were drawn up. The pedlar said nothing to William about a credit, as the latter expressly swore. Even if the stockman's story were true it did not follow that there was prearrangement. Allan Breck knew William, to whom he was as closely related as he was to James, and it would have been quite natural for him to seek funds from him. The opposition had implied that the cash James requested in his letter was intended for the deserter. The fact was that the missive mentioned neither Allan nor the purpose for which the money was needed. The very tardiness of the appeal – three days after the conjectured plotting – was enough to satisfy any uncommitted mind that there was no conspiracy.

The concealment of the two illegally owned guns was an obvious precaution, and there was nothing to suggest that the smaller, unloaded one was the killing weapon. John Beg, Dugald and the squad captain who unearthed it all verified that it was in very poor condition. John Beg told of hearing Allan Breck complain that it had misfired three times for him and worked the fourth, without hitting the blackcock he was aiming at. The fact that the two servants did not see the musket on the day of the murder did not mean that it was absent from Aucharn. It had been secreted under the girnel by Allan Oig and was found there next day. The lock of that gun was now visibly missing, Brown pointed out to the court, and it would be interesting to hear the explanation, especially as all the other exhibits had been safeguarded so punctiliously.

The jury must ignore the stockman's story that Allan Breck said James and his son would be safe if they kept their mouths shut. If one were prepared to accept that it was the truth it still would not imply that either was guilty. Some idea of John Don's trustworthiness could be gauged from his assurance to Sandy Bane that he could honestly swear that he had not handed over the French uniform; he had done nothing more blameworthy than point to where it lay.

It was cruel that the written statements of the accused's family had been used, 'more especially as it has been hitherto held to be an established principle in our law, not only that extrajudicial declarations by third parties cannot be taken or received as evidence against any pannel, but also that those who stand in the relation of wife or children to the pannel cannot be received as witnesses against him.' That James's womenfolk, from an ill-advised sense of loyalty, denied that Allan left their home in clothes belonging to their kind parent and husband added nothing to the opponents' case.

The tacksman's letter papering Breck was no diversionary tactic. It gave a faithful description and indicated where he might be caught. Its undisguised purpose was to bring about the arrest of the main suspect and his own release.

The Lord Advocate's contention that Breck's sole motive was to avenge James was contradicted by several witnesses. They gave the information that the soldier swore retribution on Glenure for supposedly reporting his presence to Crawfurd, and the colonel's oath that Glenure had told him nothing of the kind did not affect the point. Insistence by the opposing pleaders that James alone was at odds with the factor was patently untrue. Many of the Ardsheal and Lochiel tenants were in the process of being removed, and each had at least as strong a rationale as the defendant. Nor must Serjeant More Cameron be omitted, as he had said he would shoot Glenure.

All the facts brought against his client could be harmlessly interpreted. His private reputation made it hard to conceive that he would set afloat a vile crime that would gain him nothing. Irrefutable evidence showed that he was seeking a legal solution at the time of the murder. He, Brown, was confident that if the jury weighed the facts objectively, banishing from their minds all preconceived ideas, they would return a verdict of not guilty. If they found it difficult to come to such a judgment they must reach a Special Verdict, citing any circumstances that might point to the accused's innocence. (A Special Verdict was a decision that the prosecution had proved the facts of its case but that the jurors were unsure whether they added up to proof of guilt. Final adjudication and sentence were left to the judges.)

Brown sat down. The time was between seven and eight o'clock on Sunday morning. One can imagine the vast collective sigh of deliverance that breathed through the church. The talking, more than two full days of it, was done. The sleepless jurors had been obliged to fix their flagging attention on a mazy cat's-cradle of incidents, striving to follow shrewd arguments, each of which – as a Marxist might put it – seemed to carry within itself the seeds of its own contradiction. But the time for listening was past, the hour of choice at hand.

There is no record of a summing-up. Lord Cockburn in his *Circuit Journeys* recalled being told that the jury was 'very faintly admonished by Elchies, and rather encouraged by Kilkerran . . .'. The version transmitted by *By-stander*, who claimed to be in court, was more detailed. Lord Elchies, it ran, expressed sympathy for the jurymen's protracted ordeal. They were now faced with the duty of making a life or death decision. They had until eleven o'clock next morning to accomplish that solemn responsibility, a full twenty-seven hours. Before proceeding to their deliberations it might be wise to refresh their minds with sleep, and beds would be installed in their room for that purpose. The jury, choosing to disregard this advice, advanced at once to the consideration of the evidence. They were enclosed in their room where, as *By-stander* scathingly observed, they 'were pleased to refresh themselves with wine and the like . . .'. Their discussion lasted four or five hours. That afternoon young Ballachulish met one of the Campbell jurors in the street and told him that everyone was surprised that they had so speedily arrived at a verdict about such a complicated case. How had they managed it? The juror replied that they had debated only the evidence for the defence. As for the rest, 'we all had it in our heads before.'

8 The Verdict and After

THE COURT RECONVENED at the appointed hour next morning. The lengthy verdict, announced in the pedantic legal idiom of the period, proceeded to its vital declaration with a deliberation that must have seemed scarcely endurable to James. The jury unanimously found him guilty 'art and part'. The sentence of the judges was that he be hanged near the Ballachulish ferry on 8 November and his body hung in chains.

Argyll then addressed the condemned man. He had been ably defended and justly found guilty of a horrid murder. His guilt was compounded by his ingratitude to the victim, into whose trust he had insinuated himself in order to use his position to raise money for his own ends. The evictions of himself and others had spurred him to mortal hatred. The origin of the crime could be traced to the inflexible opposition of several clans, notably the Stewarts, to the ruling dynasty. In 1715 the clan had taken part in the siege of Inveraray. Four years later James himself was believed to have drawn his sword in rebellion, and in 1745 he marched with the Appin Regiment. Divine Providence sent a great prince to crush that wicked revolt. Had it succeeded, the accused and his comrades would have violated laws, liberties and the Protestant religion, shedding the blood of any clan they hated. Glenure's death was beyond question the direct consequence of the recent Rising. In the brief remainder of his life James could best serve his friends by warning them against the principles that had led him to his downfall. And might the Lord have mercy on his soul. The doomed man's reply, as given in the book of the trial some months later, went: 'My Lords, I tamely submit to my hard sentence. I forgive the jury and witnesses who have sworn several things falsely against me, and I declare, before the great God and this auditory, that I had no previous knowledge of the murder of Colin Campbell of Glenure, and am as innocent of it as a child unborn. I am not afraid to die, but what grieves me is my character, that after ages should think me capable of such a horrid and barbarous murder.'

He was taken back to his cell and the court addressed itself to the remaining items of business. The defence lawyers presented a petition on behalf of Allan Oig and his brother Charles. Invoking the much-discussed Act of 1701 they asked the court to direct the Lord Advocate either to set a date for their trial or free them. Prestongrange and Barcaldine signed a release for Charles but accepted a warrant to prepare for Allan Oig's trial. Two of the absent assizers, including Appin, were excused the payment of their fines. The other truant was probably obliged to pay up. Finally the court dealt with the woman accused of killing the child, whose case had been deferred. She entered a petition affirming her innocence and appealing for a sentence of transportation to one or other of the American colonies. Their Lordships granted the plea, stipulating that her exile should be perpetual.

The period immediately after the trial was marked by a flurry of letters among the hierarchs and others who took part in it or were concerned about its result. The excerpts and summaries which follow throw light on their reactions and reveal some background events.

25 September 1752: Prestongrange to Holdernesse
The Lord Advocate devoted much ink and space to his handling of the James More involvement, sounding a plaintive note that he had not been apprised of the memorial and signed the list of witnesses without noticing the name. The trial 'was indeed of very great importance to the future well-Government of Scotland, and especially of the highlands . . .' and because 'Justice so loudly required some vengeance or satisfaction for the murder of poor Glenure . . .'. Simon Fraser had acquitted himself well in his first court appearance. The private prosecutors had acted wisely in choosing him for the assignment, 'which Certainly will not be a grateful Circumstance to the Jacobites, to see

one whom they look upon as being the Lord Lovat, acting such a part.'

25 September 1752: Argyll to Hardwicke

'He denyed his accession to the murder with strong asseverations in answer to the exhortation I gave him, but I verily believe he is guilty, and we are all of opinion that many of his clan were privy to this murder. The strong menaces that were proved upon the prisoner had great weight with the jury together with a circumstance which is local to the Highlands, *viz.* the implacable hatred and revenge that never fails to arise when any tennants of a clan are removed to make way for strangers.'

26 September 1752: Prestongrange to Hardwicke

James was ably defended by his counsel. Most of the jurors were Campbells, but 'to get a good jury, the greater part were of that name . . .'. Not only were the main charges in the indictment established but several meaningful facts were elicited in the course of the evidence. Breck was not proved to be the killer – not unexpectedly, for there were no eyewitnesses. An account of the trial should be published in book form to quell any Jacobite complaints that James was unfairly convicted.

5 October 1752: Holdernesse to Prestongrange

He had received the Advocate's letter of 25 September and shown it to the Lords Justices, '& Their Excellencies were pleased extremely to approve your Diligence & activity in the Conduct of this very important affair; Nothing could be more material to the future well-Governing of the distant Parts of Scotland, than the exemplary Punishment of so notorious a criminal.' The verdict should persuade the disaffected to make their peace with the existing regime.

5 October 1752: Pelham to Newcastle

'P.S. I forgot to observe to you that our friends in Scotland have done extremely well, the chief villain concerned in the murder of Glenure is convicted, and will be hang'd in chains upon the spot, where the poor man was killd as soon as the Law will allow.' . . . 'The Master of Lovat was Council for the King, and pleaded strongly against Rebels, and Highland Cheiftains; not unartfull, nor unusefull, being in the face and center of their People.'

6 October 1752: Commissioners of the Treasury to Barons of the Exchequer
Simon Fraser had applied to them for arrears of a pension of £150 a year which His Majesty had been pleased to grant him out of the revenues of the forfeited estates. 'I am directed by their Lordships to desire your Lordships will be pleased to order all the arrears due to the said Simon Fraser to be immediately paid.'

8 October 1752: George Mackay (probably uncle of Glenure's widow) to Barcaldine
'I approve much of printing the Tryal.' . . . 'I and all friends have a just sense of the fatigue and trouble you must have had on this occasion, and how much the success we all wished for is oweing to your attention and Diligence . . .' . . . 'There is a Report here of such strong circumstances having come out in James Stewart's Tryal agst. his son, that he is soon to be try'd at Edinr.'

23 October 1752: Archibald Campbell to his half-brother Barcaldine
At his army posting in Limerick he had read in the English newspapers that 'one of the villains that murdered our poor brother is condemned.' . . . 'is there any hopes of hanging more of these Banditti . . .' . . . 'wont many of the poor people of that countrie be Banished how does my poor sister in law doe is she with child her situation must have been dreadful I intreat you'll write me as ffully of the Particulars of this Black affair as possible, since James Stewart's tryall has unravelled their Hellish plott.'

28 October 1752: Barons of the Exchequer to Commissioners of the Treasury

They had looked up the terms of Fraser's pension instrument and found that he was entitled to £150 per annum from the day he surrendered until the date of his pardon, and to £300 from then on. He had applied for arrears in June 1751. The document laid down that he must be paid out of the produce of the forfeited estates, and it was impossible to know if there would be a profit after debts and expenses were settled. Their Lordships suggested that the Treasury authorise them to pay the arrears out of Lord Elcho's estate, which was certain to yield a large profit.

5 November 1752: Breadalbane to Hardwicke

'Stuart who is condemn'd has since confess'd that he wish'd for the murder of Mr Campbell and expected it would have been committed sooner, but still denies his knowing it at the time it was committed. This Confession agrees with Allan Breck Stuart's having been seen hovering about the road to Edinburgh, from whence Mr Campbell was returning after making his report to the Barons of the Exchequer, but happening to go another way, Breck miss'd him back into the Countrey.' . . . '. . . nothing but rough measures will do in that Countrey.'

The Campbells, prosecutors and politicians celebrated the verdict with varying degrees of satisfaction. Barcaldine was wreathed in congratulations, not least from King George, who had followed developments keenly. Meanwhile James contemplated his ignoble extinction in his cell at Inveraray. A right of appeal did not then exist. Only a royal pardon could save him, but a petition to the king begging clemency for a former rebel convicted of killing a Crown official would have been a waste of paper. His jailers took elaborate steps to prevent his escape or violent extrication. Guards were doubled and strangers from Appin and Lochaber compelled to account for their presence in town. The prisoner was attended by a local minister, Alexander

128

Campbell. *By-stander* relates that before administering the holy sacrament the clergyman solemnly emphasised the need for confession and repentance. He put the plain question: 'Are you guilty of the murder of Glenure?' The reply came: 'I am not guilty of it, even in the smallest degree. If I be, may this which I am about to do, tend to my eternal damnation.' It was not death that oppressed his mind, he said, but the prospect of leaving his wife and family in poverty. He owned no land, and his savings had been consumed by the cost of the trial. Posterity's view of him as a convicted murderer greatly saddened him, he told visitors. His lawyers brought solace with the assurance that they had kept notes of their speeches with the intention of publishing a book of the trial. 'If that shall be done,' said James, 'the world will have an opportunity of seeing and judging of my share in the murder, a crime I ever abhorred, and the justice done me in the trial.'

His son Charles was released on the last day of September. On 5 October eighty troopers took the road to Fort William with the bound and mounted tacksman. What seem like excessive security measures were in fact fully justified. The Jacobites, inevitably sickened by the verdict, hurled accusations of jury-rigging, bribery and perjured witnesses. To their eyes James already glowed in a martyr's nimbus. The possibility of a rescue attempt on the road north could not be discounted, for the transfer of the prisoner entailed four or five days' travel through remote regions where the king's writ was not enthusiastically respected. The journey passed off uneventfully but the theme of rescue cropped up later, as will be seen.

With James safely reincarcerated, Stonefield set in train preparations for the execution. He called on the aid of the sheriff of Inverness in the task of constructing a gibbet, and they turned their attention to purchasing timber and iron in Maryburgh. Iron was required to plate the wooden beams, the Crown lawyers having recommended it to prevent James's friends from cutting down the gibbet and recovering the body. The sheriffs encountered considerable reluctance among tradesmen to undertake work of this nature – an understandable posture in a village full of Camerons and Stewarts – but they finally succeeded in hiring enough workmen to fashion the grim apparatus. As there was no resident hangman in Argyll at that time they engaged one from Inverness. Stonefield then returned to Inveraray and employed a blacksmith to forge the chains in which the corpse was to be hung. He next journeyed to Glasgow to recruit a second executioner, lest the Inverness craftsman should become unavailable for one reason or another.

Of James's last month in the fort we know next to nothing. He received spiritual consolation from ministers of the district, and we can safely assume that his family and friends were permitted to see him frequently. A report of one man's talk with the prisoner has come down to us in the *Journals of the Episcopal Visitations of the Right Rev. Robert Forbes, MA*. Many years after the murder the bishop spent some time at Ballachulish House at the invitation of the laird's son. He was told, almost certainly by young Ballachulish, though he does not say so, that a Cameron visited the condemned cell and informed James of a plot to liberate him. A party of fifty Camerons was to descend on his escorting guards as he was being transferred to the place of execution. Having put them to flight they would make off with James and spirit him to a secure refuge. The scheme was firmly vetoed by the prisoner. It would inflict more damage on his country than his life was worth, he ruled, and he did not wish to hear another word about it. That such a conversation occurred is doubtful – it bears a suspect whiff of hagiolatry – but it is not beyond the limit of possibility. The Camerons were renowned for their daring. Bishop Forbes was shown the spot where the ambush was purposed and concluded that it might well have been rewarded with success.

The execution site was a lofty, grass-topped hump of rock near the ferry. A few days before the scheduled date Stonefield arrived to supervise the erection of the gibbet. He was protected by a small mounted detail, and may have been accompanied by the Glasgow hangman and the blacksmith with his chains. They were joined by the sheriff of Inverness and the Maryburgh artisans, the carpenters bearing the gibbet and the smith his iron panels. It is likely that the other executioner came with them. The gibbet was fixed in position and plated. On Tuesday, 7 November James was convoyed by a hundred soldiers on his last journey to Appin. The two ministers bore him company. When they reached the ferry the wind was blowing so fiercely that they could not cross. The next morning was 'very Boisterous and wett', to quote Stonefield's report, but the short passage was accomplished without mishap shortly after midday. On the rocky knoll a sail was pressed into service as an improvised tent, and James and the clergymen occupied it for a little time. A number of local folk had gathered for a final leave-taking. Among them was Charles Stewart, the notary who had twice left the dying man in the lurch. His is the only spectator's name of which there is any record, but we are told that the execution was attended by those of the convicted man's family and friends who could face the harrowing scene. The wind blew so savagely that they could scarcely keep their feet, and the tent was 'destroyed', probably whipped away.

The ministers said a short prayer. James produced three copies of a speech and gave one to Stonefield and another to the captain of the guard. He asked permission to read aloud the third, which was granted. Then in a clear, confident voice he read his last declaration. His reasons for making this statement, he began, were to reveal that his innocence made his suffering bearable; to forestall the accusations of guilt which silence on such an occasion might provoke; to disclose the illegalities that had crippled his defence; to deny a rumour spread by the lawmen that he had confessed; and to offer advice to his friends and relations. He emphatically denied knowing anything of the murder. He now suspected Allan Breck in response to information that had come out after Glenure's death. His motives for sending the money were natural affection for a kinsman he had reared and gratitude

131

for Allan's loyalty to Ardsheal, whom he partnered when the laird went into hiding after Culloden.

He knew nothing of Breck's borrowing his clothes nor of his movements after leaving Aucharn on 12 May. The subject of killing the factor had never arisen between them. The tenants had indeed requested him to act for them, and their subsequent denials were prompted by fear of the prosecutors. John Don's testimony that James said he would drag himself to Glenure's window to take a shot at him was a lie. He could not recall telling his Maccoll servants that Red Colin meant to make himself laird of Appin, or that there had once been commoners in the country who would not allow the man to carry on as he was doing. 'But this I can safely say, that John Beg Maccoll came in to the gaol at Inveraray to see me the next day after my sentence was passed, crying and tearing as if he was half-mad, and told me that the night Dougal Maccoll and he himself were on their way to Inveraray, at the strath of Appin, Ewen Roy Maccoll, portioner of Glassdrim, and the said John More Maccoll, brought two bottles of aqua vitae into the barn where they were confined, and wrought upon them to make up that story, and made them believe that it could not hurt me, and would gain them friendship at Barcaldine's hand.'

Sandy Bane told several lies, the greatest of which was that James tried to set up a cash credit for Breck. Bribes were freely offered, Ballachulish's herdsman being tempted with a hundred pounds. The miller at Ardsheal, one of the tenants due for eviction, was promised that he could retain his lease if he made any serviceable revelations.

After listing the ploys designed to hinder a successful defence James took up some of the charges against him. He had not been 'out' in 1715 and 1719, as he had been too young, and he had been pardoned for his part in the 'Forty-five. The errors of his forefathers were quoted to blacken his character in a courtroom full of men who themselves had been in rebellion at one time or another, or whose families had been. Then there was the surprising accusation that he looked after widows and orphans, a practice that gained him much influence. 'I hope soon to appear before a Judge who will reward charity and benevolence in a different way; and I only regret how little service was in my power to do, not only to the fatherless and widows, but to all mankind in general, as I thank God I would make all the race of Adam happy if I could.' One charge to which he did plead guilty was that of collecting surplus rents, but Glenure was aware of the donations and consented to them. The money was used solely for the upkeep of the impoverished children of his loving and generous brother.

He had never confessed to the murder, being innocent. The Inveraray minister was the only person who asked him that question, and James could not believe that it was he who had spread the slander. 'It is very true that I told Mr Campbell I had no personal love for Glenure, and that I was sorry how few in his neighbourhood had. But I hope no man would construct that as if I had an intention to murder him.'

The jury approached the trial with a predetermined conviction of his guilt. That was made evident by their two interruptions of Mr Brown's closing address. James understood that this did not often happen in Christian countries, but at least the incidents revealed that he had been marked down for sacrifice, whoever was the culprit. His remark to the Campbell innkeeper that there was nothing to which he would help any of his name except the gallows was – on the word of a Christian facing eternity – a joke. If he had harboured hatred for the clan there was no need for him to enter that inn as 'there was another public-house within a gunshot of his door.' Of his horseback conversation with Colin Maclaren he could not recall one word, as he was very drunk. He freely forgave those witnesses and the jury, and entreated his friends and family to do likewise. They must endure with resignation the destruction of his character by his prosecutors, contenting themselves with the knowledge that he was free of guilt. He called on God to protect them, to lead them in the paths of peace, and grant them a joyful reunion in the hereafter. Mr Campbell the minister, whose kindly advice he much appreciated, had told him that fear of compromising his friends might prevent his divulging all he knew about the crime. He now therefore declared that to the best of his information none of them encompassed the murder, nor could he bring himself to conceive that any was so lacking in humanity as to shoot the gentleman from a bush. He held the opinion that if Allan Breck was the murderer he acted alone.

'I die an unworthy member of the Episcopal Church of Scotland, as established before the Revolution, in full charity with all mortals, sincerely praying God may bless all my friends and relations, benefactors and well-wishers, particularly my poor wife and children, who in a special manner I recommend to His divine care and protection; and may the same God pardon and forgive all that ever did or wished me evil, as I do from my heart forgive them. I die in full hopes of mercy, not through any merit in myself, as I freely own I merit no good at the hands of my offended God; but my hope is through the blood, merits, and mediation of the ever-blessed Jesus, my Redeemer and glorious Advocate, to whom I recommend my spirit. Come, Lord Jesus, come quickly.' In a postscript he added: 'Mr Coupar, minister, showed me some queries a few days ago which he was desired to put to me. They are all answered already in my speech, excepting two, which are – Whether I knew Allan Breck's route from Ballachelish to Koalisnacoan, and from thence to Rannoch, before the murder happened? Answer – I declare before God I did not. – Whether I interceded with James Drummond, in the Tolbooth of Edinburgh, to persuade or entice his brother Robert, who was already outlawed, to murder Glenure, and that I would give him a good gun for that purpose, and money for carrying him off the country, and that Ardsheal's interest would procure him a commission on France? Answer – I declare before God there never passed such words betwixt James More Drummond and me, or any proposal to that effect.'

James signed the speech and gave it to the sheriff. Stonefield addressed the condemned man, voicing surprise that he had made statements which he, the sheriff, knew to be untrue. As time was short he would mention only one. James had complained that there were two interruptions of his lawyer's speech to the jury. The truth was that one juryman asked Mr Brown to be as brief as possible, as the trial had lasted so long. Two others then rose to assure the advocate that they would hear him out, at whatever length. Charles Stewart the notary spoke up to confirm Stonefield's recollection, thus failing to support James for the third time. Or in biblical parlance, he denied him thrice. The tacksman said he had interpreted the incident differently and was sorry if he had said anything that was not true. He knelt down and read Psalm 35, an apposite choice. 'For without cause have they hid for me their net in a pit, which without cause they have digged for my soul.' . . . 'Yea, they opened their mouth wide against me, and said, Aha, aha, our eye hath seen it.' He bade a last goodbye to his friends, calmly climbed the ladder, read a short prayer, and was 'turned off', in the gruesome slang of the era. Within a few minutes the trials of James of the Glen came to an end.

The wild weather having delayed the proceedings, it was five o'clock before the blacksmith hung the body in chains and the onlookers turned for home through the gloaming. Margaret probably stayed overnight at Ballachulish House. She had bought sugar and a quarter-pound of tea on the previous day, presumably to serve to sympathisers at the wake. The laird had laid in six bottles of wine and spirits and a barrel of coal. No doubt his fires burned late as the mourners drank to the memory of the man whose corpse was visible from the windows.

9 Postscripts

FIFTEEN SOLDIERS were detailed to mount constant guard over the body. The place of execution had been chosen for its proximity to the scene of the crime and its conspicuous site. All who walked the high road between Appin and Glencoe were obliged to pass the gibbet, and the elevated location made it discernible to Camerons living along an extensive stretch of Lochs Linnhe and Leven. It could be seen from Callert House, the home of the dead man's half-sister Helen. No Jacobite was to be left uncertain of the fate of anyone convicted of killing a King's factor.

A week after the hanging James More Drummond escaped from Edinburgh Castle by means of a ruse that struck Scotland with astonishment and mirth. His tall daughter Elizabeth donned men's clothes, sporting a floppy hat that concealed her face. With a pair of shoes in her hand she succeeded in talking her way into the rogue's cell, posing as a cobbler. Father and daughter swapped clothes. The guards outside the room heard voices raised in a simulated slanging-match. The door was flung open and James More, his face half-hidden by the hat, strode to freedom, shoes in hand, mouthing expletives about his supposedly dissatisfied customer. The jailers soon tumbled to the trick. The castle was ransacked and the city gates shut, to no avail. Next day he brazenly called at a gentleman's house. On being asked why he had made his incriminating statement about James he insisted that every word of it was true. 'This makes a great noise,' wrote Breadalbane to Barcaldine on the following day, 'and I'm told the Jacobites say it was connived at by the D. of Arg. and the Adv. for offering his evidence against James Stewart, whereas neither the D. nor the Adv. have any influence in the Castle.' He informed another correspondent: 'This James Drummond the Sunday after his Escape went publickly to Church in Balquidder a Countrey belonging to the Duke of Montrose,

136

& after the Service gave an account of his Escape to many of the Congregation, & then retired to his hiding place. He dares not go among his old friends the Stewarts, they being now his declared enemies on account of James Stewart.' Oddly enough the breakout may have been unnecessary, for Prestongrange had a grudging regard for the Macgregor and could well have pulled strings to save him. Although he described him as the head of the worst family of the worst clan in the Highlands he wondered if the public interest would best be served by executing a man of his natural talents, boldness and address. He might more usefully be deported to the frontiers of Nova Scotia, the Advocate had mused, taking a number of his family and tribe with him. The general public too were not totally unsympathetic. In an age in many ways cruder than our own some felt that, compared with earlier misdeeds of the clan, the trifling matter of abduction and rape was just a piece of high-spirited tomfoolery.

The scoundrel's operatic exit was differently interpreted by the champions of the tacksman's innocence and his decriers. The Campbells hailed James More's repetition of his charge as proof that he was telling the truth, reasoning that the fact that he risked his life to do so, at a time when he was beyond the reach of punishment or reward, scotched the accusation that he dreamed up his story to save himself from the long drop. The Jacobites saw the escape as a charade staged to pay off a useful stooge, and their suspicions were further excited by the jail-breaker's public appearance on his home territory. The demotion of three soldiers, including two officers, and the whipping of the jail porter may have served to allay scepticism.

Three weeks after the execution the address from the scaffold was published, creating intense interest. The contending factions reacted predictably. 'I saw Steward's speech,' commented Glenure's widow Janet, 'which is but a very poor one in the opinion of most people. I hope his Tryalls will convince mainie of his Guilt when they are come out of the Print.' Enemies of the House of Hanover saluted it as the testament of a fighter for the royal line

137

whose name he bore, and blameless victim of a usurping tyranny. The impact of James's dying words on uncommitted readers can only be guessed, but no one can have remained unaffected by the remarkable declaration. The lofty diction of his affirmation of faith, the final slur on Glenure's reputation, his naming of false witnesses and his forgiveness of the accusers cannot have failed to evoke turbulent and contradictory emotions. His use of the expression 'within a gunshot of his door' must have raised many a startled eyebrow, considering the manner of the victim's death. His admission that he could not recall a word of his drunken conversation with Colin Maclaren undoubtedly touched everyone who had ever tippled to the point of amnesia – surely a numerous category – with a throb of fellow-feeling.

Breadalbane was not in two minds about the effect of the speech. He quoted the view that James, 'a notoriously hardy fellow', refused to confess through fear of the consequences to Allan Oig and possibly others. The choleric earl was certain that the address which, he said, was believed to have been composed by a clergyman, could make little impression on impartial minds. He observed that the publication had aroused extraordinary attention and stirred the opposition to renewed and openly aired charges of malpractice. To a correspondent he confided: 'Stewart's dying speech . . . makes a great noise here & the Jacobites say publickly that the witnesses were bribed, & that all who swore against him were corrupted & perjured. I wish the Trial had been printed, which (as I'm inform'd) would have shewd the contrary so plain that no Credit could be given to such Insinuations which are now very much believed.' He wrote to Barcaldine: 'I have seen Js. Stewart's last speech; which I think makes it more necessary to print the Trial.' His opinion may have been reinforced by London newspapers which nudged their readers with innuendoes stressing the location of the trial and the identity of the presiding judge. The proposal to publish had been mooted by Prestongrange just after the trial ended and, as we have seen, welcomed by the defence team. The Advocate consulted the Lord Chancellor, Hardwicke, who passed responsibility for the decision to Argyll. The duke at first opposed the project but then relented, stipulating that only the official court records and counsel's speeches should go to press, thereby preventing a pamphlet battle over what was actually said. Several extraneous remarks had been made, he argued, which would merely baffle an English reader. Publication was set in motion. Argyll declined the drudgery of reproducing from memory his address to the condemned man, leaving it to others who had been present. *By-stander* was to snarl that 'the speech spoke was much more acute and bitter than the speech printed.' The advocates set about turning their notes into flowing Ciceronian prose, and on 30 December Prestongrange let it be known that some of the material for the book was already at the printer's and that he himself was on the point of writing his speeches.

On 11 December Allan Oig was released from the fort. What few facts are available suggest that the authorities were far from persuaded of his innocence but lacked sufficient evidence to put him in the dock. The joy Margaret must have felt on welcoming her son home was soon followed by a grievous disappointment. Shortly after Christmas she received a suit of clothes she had ordered from her brother William. It was intended as a burial cerement for James, whose corpse she seems to have hoped would be restored to her. The squad guarding the gallows requested, and was supplied with, a hut furnished with beds and utensils to shelter them from the rigours of winter – an unmistakable signal that their stay would be a long one.

A month later the other widow, Janet Campbell, suffered vexation arising from a very different cause; she gave birth to a daughter. '. . . you won't be surprised when I tell you,' she wrote to her brother-in-law Sheriff Duncan, 'this Disappointment sitts Heavie on me, and greatly adds to the many afflictions I have mett with. There is no helping such, but to Submit cheerfully to the will of God, who orders all for the best, and not as mankind.' She went on to warn him not to credit the wicked rumours that she and her father had planned to substitute a boy for the daughter. It was true that they had joked about it, but with no serious intent. She offered her opinion that the slander emanated 'from the friends of that wretch who was executed . . .'. The baby was named Colina. In the autumn of 1753 Janet remarried, to the fury of her father, who had not been consulted. In the years that ensued she wrote several times to Duncan, now laird of Glenure, soliciting money for the upkeep and education of her daughters. His response was so meagre that her father took up the cudgels on her behalf, and the result was a prolonged and rancorous rift between the families.

In February 1753 *Trial of James Stewart* went on sale at a price of five shillings. Crawfurd sourly commented that the book merely confirmed the prejudices each reader brought to it. Unbiased scrutineers came to the conclusion that James was guilty, he maintained. He jibbed at the book's version of the accused's reply to Argyll's closing address: it quoted him to the effect that he was as innocent as the babe unborn, a simile he did not use. A few months later *A Supplement to the Trial of James Stewart by a By-stander* led off with a complaint that none of the official documents had been reproduced in the book and continued for eighty-three pages with a fierce dissection of the prosecution case. It concluded by appealing to its readers to agree that James had been in essence murdered. *By-stander*'s trenchant booklet is said to have provoked retaliatory broadsheets which the present author has been unable to trace. If they existed it seems reasonable to suppose that they followed the general lines of the *Justification*. Its main arguments, apart from those quoted in previous pages, can be enumerated briefly:

1 James's claim that one of the Barons, Kennedy, had advised the tenants to resist eviction was a falsehood. It was the Barons themselves who had empowered Glenure to lease and eject. Who could put faith in any utterance of a man who told so palpable a lie?

2   When precognosed, Donald Stewart swore that he had no
     contact with Breck after the midday of the crime. In court
     he stated that he met him that evening, 'and if I am not
     misinformed Mr Stewart of Edinglassie is no stranger to the
     cause that made the difference so glaring.'
3   The complaint that James More Drummond's name had been
     listed among the prosecution witnesses came strangely from
     the defender of a man who thought highly enough of the
     Macgregor to visit him in jail.
4   The charge that the authorities suppressed documents exhib-
     ited in court is answered by the very fact that these were
     evidence for the *prosecution*.
5   That there was a wide-ranging conspiracy was as clear as
     day, and Glenure was only its first target. His murderers mis-
     takenly reckoned that his successor would not dare to lease
     forfeited property to anyone but friends of the dispossessed
     lairds. They were now crying out against the prosecutors of
     one of the killers in order to pave the way for further protest
     if any of his abettors should come to trial.
     There were no more trials. Though nothing remotely resem-
bling actionable evidence surfaced after the execution the peace
officers clung to their fixation that many heads had come together
in the affair. Their flickering hopes may have been rekindled by
the capture of Serjeant More Cameron in April of 1753. He went
to the gallows without disclosing any knowledge of the murder. A
month after his arrest Cameron of Fassiefern was imprisoned on
a charge of treasonable correspondence with attainted persons.
One of his co-defendants was Charles Stewart, writer in Banavie,
in all probability James's broken reed. Colonel Crawfurd, who
made no secret of his zeal to remove the belligerent Fassiefern,
proposed to produce witnesses who would swear that he tried to
stir them to murder Glenure and threaten his wife. Prestongrange
declared with satisfaction that this would hang the man or at least
exile him to Nova Scotia – apparently the Advocate's favourite
oubliette for troublemakers. The witnesses did not come forward

and the charges were dropped. Almost at once a fresh indictment was drawn up, this time the charge being forgery. A verdict of guilty was returned in January 1755. Fassiefern was banished for ten years to Alnwick in Northumberland and Charles Stewart was disbarred from practice as a public notary.

James never wore his grave-clothes. For years his corpse was lashed by gales and shrivelled by the sun. After eighteen months its military custodians were recalled to other duties. In January 1755 the cadaver fell to the ground and an official enquiry concluded that the incident was caused by high winds. The Lord Justice-Clerk ordered that the bones should be reconnected by wire clips and the remains restored to the gibbet. The skeleton slowly disintegrated. Local tradition relates that the younger Ballachulish gathered each bone as it fell, and eventually laid them all in the coffin with the body of Margaret, who had not long outlived her husband. The grave is in a corner of the roofless old church at Keil, where the Ardsheals were by custom laid to rest. Its ancient name, Kilchallumchille, ('the church of Challumchille'), hints at the possible presence of St Columba, the founder of Derry and Iona, and missionary to the Picts. A plate let into the wall records the last resting place of 'Seumas a' Ghlinne'. At the foot of the grave lies another, marked by a long recumbent slate on which is incised: 'Sacred to the MEMORY of Dougald McColl late Tenant at Cuil who Departed this life 22d of April 1813 aged 84 years and Catherine McCorquodale his Spouse. Memento Mori.' James's labourer Dugald gave his age at the trial as twenty-four. Assuming that his birthday fell in the five months from the end of April, the dates fit. There were many Dugalds, or Dougalds, in Appin, and many Maccolls, but there is more than a chance that they are the same man. A few miles away, in Lettermore Wood, the spot where Glenure perished is marked by a memorial cairn. It is only a long gunshot from the grassy eminence, now crowned with shrubs and trees, where James died. The occasion is commemorated by a simple monument erected by the Stewart Society. A rugged quartzite boulder, roughly cubic, and said to be the one James liked to sit on while supervising his workers in the fields, rests on a stone plinth. A few inscribed words record his execution 'for a crime of which he was not guilty'.

Scarcely anything is known of the destinies of James and Margaret's children. *Inveraray Papers* states that after the tacksman's death an effort was made to persuade Allan Oig to put himself forward as his father's heir, but he refused. His motive seems to have been the avoidance of responsibility for James's debts. The same authority affirms that in 1755 Mungo Campbell took legal action against him for rent arrears incurred by his father. No public reference to Allan Oig's later life has come to view, and his name does not crop up in the rich folklore that burgeoned around the tragedy. This silence suggests that he may have left the district to start life afresh. His brother Charles likewise vanished from official history, but the story has been handed down that he practised his shoemaking trade in Edinburgh, where he died. Bishop Forbes met one of the daughters in Maryburgh twenty years after the murder. The unmarried milliner may well have been Peggy, who was probably James's younger girl, for the only extant bill from her uncle William shows her to have been much preoccupied with her wardrobe.

Janet Campbell's eldest daughter Elizabeth died young. Lucy married a relative while still in her teens, had twenty-one children and lived into her eighties. Colina, who is said to have closely resembled her father, married James Baillie, a trader with the West Indies and a slave-owner. He decided to stand for Parliament and is believed to have paid the going rate of £5000 for his candidature in the 1790 election to a magnate at Horsham, a rotten borough which sent two Members to Westminster. Another magnate entered his own brace of candidates, and the campaign was conducted on both sides with a degree of knavery uncommon even in the malodorous politicking of the day. Baillie and his running-mate lost and appealed to Parliament. A committee ruled that the election was invalid and that Baillie and

143

his partner were the lawful MPs. He took his seat and used the House as a pulpit to defend the institution of slavery. Curiously, his running-mate, Lord William Gordon, was a distant cousin of Lord Byron, and one of the unseated MPs was Timothy Shelley, the father of Percy Bysshe Shelley.

Barcaldine continued as factor on the Perth estate until 1765. He pursued his duties energetically, evincing much concern for the lessees under his management, and was never bird-mouthed about offering impatient advice to his masters. He secured their blessing for his scheme to rent farms to disabled ex-soldiers, but the project proved unworkable. He was dismissed from his post for unlawfully accepting presents from the tenants and for tardiness in submitting his accounts, which differed widely from the calculations of the Inspector General. His personal finances too became chaotic and he ran into serious debt. He was reduced to selling his estate to his half-brother Sheriff Duncan, who thus became laird of Barcaldine and Glenure. The landless man died in 1777, as old as the century. His son Mungo took on the additional burden of the factorships of Barrisdale and Kinlochmoidart in 1753. With a squad of army bodyguards now at his disposal he soon showed that he would brook no defiance from his tenants. He accepted a challenge from a Knoydart Cameron and travelled to fight in that hostile region, an exploit that led Breadalbane to huff that he must not behave like a Don Quixote tilting at Jacobite windmills. In a further display of firmness Mungo confiscated a quantity of kelp illegally burned by young Callert. Yet he was compassionate enough to appeal to the Barons not to evict the widowed and penniless Helen Cameron and her clutch of young children. Mrs Grant of Laggan, a popular versifier and belletrist, is quoted as describing him as a man 'whose warm and generous heart, whose enlightened and comprehensive mind, whose social and public virtues I should delight to commemorate did my limits permit'. On entering his thirties he ventured on a military career and engaged in action against the French in Canada. Six years later he was transferred to Ireland, remaining there until the outbreak of the American War of Independence. On 6 October 1777 Lieutenant-Colonel Campbell led his regiment in the attack on Fort Montgomery. The defending militiamen had spiked the approaches with an obstructive ring of boulders and felled trees. Long-range shots were exchanged for most of the afternoon. At five o'clock Mungo advanced under a flag of truce and demanded the surrender of the fort. The Americans gave him a dusty answer. Battle recommenced and, in the musket-fire and grapeshot from the rebels, Mungo received his death from the barrel of a gun, like his uncle.

Simon Fraser too deserted the law in answer to the headier call of arms. The erstwhile Master of Lovat created Fraser's Highlanders, a regiment more than a thousand strong, recruited from his own clan. While serving under Wolfe in Canada he was twice wounded in the advance on Quebec. In 1762 he sailed with the British expedition to Portugal, in whose army he was commissioned as a major-general. When the Americans rebelled he raised two battalions to form the 71st Regiment, which gave a good account of itself. Fraser himself did not take part in the war. He became the first president of the Highland Society of London and agitated, with success, for the repeal of the Act forbidding Highland dress. His labours for the nation were recognised by the restoration of his lands. The Lieutenant-General died childless at the age of fifty-five, lauded in official panegyrics, unmourned in the crofts of Appin. Fraser had his admirers, but Mrs Grant was not of their number. 'A slight veil of decorum was thrown over the turpitude of his heart and conduct,' she judged, 'and he was a well-bred, shrewd, plausible man and a good enough soldier.' ... 'He was too much a man of sense and of the world to forsake the straight path openly, yet no heart was ever harder, or no hand more rapacious than his.'

Old Ballachulish lived to be ninety. A few years before his death Bishop Forbes described him as 'the old, trusty Trojan' who was 'one of the most chearful distinct old Persons I ever conversed with'. In his later years he prospered greatly from

145

the development of slate quarries on his land. His son John lived until 1794, a fluent raconteur of rebel yarns and judge of bagpipe competitions, when the estate passed into the hands of his only child, daughter Lilias.

Eluding every watchful eye, Allan Breck stepped ashore in France ten months after the murder. So said Robin Macgregor, who returned from the Continent soon after Breck arrived. The soldier had told him that Allan Oig was the murderer and that he, Breck, was going to write a self-exculpating statement. That Allan reached France in March was confirmed by Robin's brother, James More. The prison-breaker, by his own report, took ship from Scotland soon after his escape. He put in briefly in the Isle of Man, spent some time in Ireland, then landed in France in May, 1753. A month later he wrote to Barcaldine with the news that Breck had rejoined his regiment and was being shunned by his comrades. James More was impressing on exiled Scots that James Stewart's trial had been fair, and in defending Glenure's reputation he had been forced to draw his sword against a fellow-countryman, 'who I believe will give no further trouble for some time comming'. If Barcaldine could procure a warrant for Breck's arrest James More would organise it. He proposed to inveigle the slippery outlaw into Holland, where some English Campbells would help with the seizure. Parties to the plot should carry torn halves of playing cards for identification. As a quid pro quo – though James was too sly to put it so baldly – he asked Barcaldine to intercede for his brother Robin, who had been captured. He would hang if Barcaldine and his friends did not prompt Breadalbane to use his influence to have the sentence commuted to banishment. James twice wrote to the earl on the same tack, declaring himself willing to visit him to discuss it. Breadalbane refused all contact. Much as he yearned to lay Breck by the heels he knew that if he were to meet James More, there could be no telling what kind of distorted version of the interview the mountebank might circulate. Barcaldine also warily rebuffed him.

146

At the same time James was corresponding with other Campbells, including – if we can trust the Macgregor's account – Sheriff Duncan. They sent over a representative who talked the British ambassador in Paris into applying for a safe-conduct pass for James. This was obtained and plans laid for the kidnap of Allan Breck. Then two Scotsmen alerted him to the danger. James More later lamented that on the very night he reckoned to seize Breck the soldier fled, pausing only long enough to rob James's trunk of some clothes and four snuff-boxes. James went to London to plead for Robin's life and his own pardon. Under questioning by Hardwicke and Holdernesse he gave details of the manoeuvrings of Prince Charles, and alleged that a fresh rebellion was astir. According to James, Holdernesse offered him a well-paid official post, conceivably his former niche as a Government stool-pigeon. He declined it, saying that it was inconsistent with the sense of honour of one who had been born in the character of a gentleman. Robin was hanged for a murder he had committed some years before, and James was deported to France. There he learned that Allan Breck had sworn to kill him if he showed his face in the country again. A few months later James More fell ill and died with his boots off, probably to the surprise of some.

The rest of Breck's career can be pieced together with the help of documents which the present narrator managed to uncover in the French army records. It is certain that he left Ogilvy's Regiment soon after he rejoined it in 1753, for by 1757 he had attained officer rank in another, Bouillon's. A year later Barcaldine was alerted to a rumour that he was in Balquhidder but nothing came of it. An Appin legend pictures him in action against Wolfe's troops in Canada in the following year. This is not inherently improbable, but the story is told with so many folkloric grace notes that it must be regarded as very doubtful. Four years later, in the course of a large-scale reorganisation and contraction of the army, Breck was laid off the strength of Bouillon's. A list of the regimental pensions dated 13 April

1763 records among the second captains: 'Allan Stuart 500' (*livres*). He enlisted in the Lyonnais Regiment, which in turn was reconstructed in 1777. From its papers of that year comes this translated entry:

Allan Stuart,
released from the service

The Military Merit Cross
Reported to have commenced his service in Scotland as a captain by right of birth in the regiment of the Stuarts of Appin whose colonel was M. de Stuart Dardshelle, the officers of which had been promised by the late King that those who fought under the flag of Prince Edouard should retain their rank if they came to France.

The *sieur* Allan Stuart came here to resume his service as a private in Ogilvy in 1748, and since then was appointed as a senior lieutenant in Bouillon in 1763.

Readers will note that the soldier, in a statement whose early details can have come only from himself, claimed closer kinship with Appin or Ardsheal than the facts admit, upgraded himself to a captaincy in the Appin contingent and backdated his enrolment in Ogilvy's by a year. The Military Merit Cross, however, was a prestigious award for valour in war which no amount of bluff could have gained him if he had not proved his mettle in the field. At one stage its numbers were limited to twenty-five. The present author has failed to locate Breck's enrolment in either Bouillon or Lyonnais, and concluded that he joined both units under a *nom de guerre*. The practice was widespread. Indeed, Lyonnais seem to have insisted that their recruits submit a battlefield nickname in addition to a conventional forename and surname, a requirement that led to some waggish entries like Bellefleur and Aimable. To Allan Breck, glancing over his shoulder for the shadow of an avenging Campbell, such pseudonymity would have been simple common sense. He probably reverted to his

William Grant of Prestongrange, Lord Advocate of Scotland

Archibald Campbell, 3rd Duke of Argyll
'. . . *anybody could hang a guilty man, but only
the head of Clan Campbell an innocent one*'.

Alan Thomson

James Stewart's burial place, Keil Chapel
'Where the Ardsheals were by custom laid to rest'.

Simon Fraser, formerly Master of Lovat

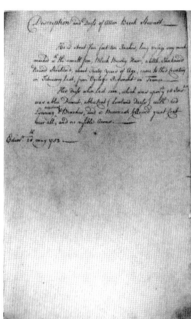

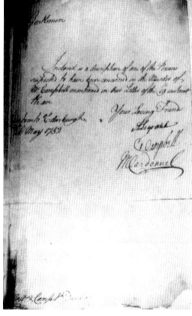

Custom's correspondence regarding
Allan Breck Stewart, 1752

By kind permission of HM Customs & Excise

Approach to Glenure's Memorial

James Stewart's Monument, Ballachulish

Auchindarroch in Glen Duror

given name only when the questions of pensions and honours arose, his Highland pride dictating that the certificate inscrolling his military prowess should record his true identity.

After his departure from the Lyonnais in 1777 it is against all the odds that he continued soldiering. In his mid fifties, and scarcely prime recruiting material, he may have felt that thirty-odd years under arms had been enough to earn him a chair by the chimney-breast. A decade later he made his only known undisputable public appearance in France. Alexander Campbell, younger of Ardchattan, a grand-nephew of Glenure, was at the time avoiding his creditors by roving the Continent, capturing its scenic beauties with pencil and paintbrush. In a letter dated 26 June 1787 the talented spendthrift told his father: 'I also saw another person whom I did not believe was in the land of the living. I went down the Seine a few days ago to Paris to meet a Gentleman that intended coming here to spend some months. I was only two days in Town and lodged at the Grand Hotel D'Orleans where there is a table d'hote very cheap and of course frequented by all the Gentlemen of the sword: the second day while I was in my room writing there came in a tall thin ugly Man who said he was my Country Man and was desirous of my acquaintance. He told me his name was Stewart, and that he was from Appin; that he generally went under the name of Allan Breck in that country and was suspected of having murdered my uncle Glenuir. You may believe of course I was not a little surprised with such an introduction and wished to get quit of him as soon as possible: he denied the murder and swore by all that was sacred it was not him, that he knew who it was, but was bound by oath to conceal it, but that the world would know it after his death by his papers. He had been in the French service ever since he fled the Country and is now a Capt: on half pay and a Chevalier of St Louis.'

An anecdote that has attracted considerable disbelief is narrated by Sir Walter Scott in the Appendix to *Rob Roy*. 'About 1789 a friend of mine, then residing at Paris, was invited to see

149

some procession which was supposed likely to interest him, from the windows of an appartment occupied by a Scottish Benedictine priest. He found, sitting by the fire, a tall, thin, raw-boned, grim-looking old man with the petit croix of St Louis. His visage was strongly marked by the irregular projection of the cheek-bones and chin. His eyes were grey. His grizzled hair exhibited marks of having been red, and his complexion was weather-beaten, and remarkably freckled. Some civilities in French passed between the old man and my friend, in the course of which they talked of the streets and squares of Paris, till at length the old soldier, for such he seemed, and such he was, said with a sigh, in a sharp Highland accent, "Deil ane o' them is worth the Hie Street of Edinburgh!" On enquiry, this admirer of Auld Reekie, which he was never to see again, proved to be Allan Breck Stewart. He lived decently on his little pension, and had, in no subsequent period of his life, shown anything of the savage mood in which he is generally believed to have assassinated the enemy and oppressor, as he supposed him, of his family and clan.' This encounter has been labelled apocryphal on the basis that Breck had dark hair and eyes, and that there never existed an Order of the Petite Croix of St Louis. As has been mentioned, the army records show that his eyes were indeed grey. The fact that a fire had been lit indicates the possibility that the day was far advanced and the light failing. If so, Scott's friend could have been deceived as to the colour of the old man's hair by the play of firelight on it. He might likewise have mistaken Breck's pocks for freckles. It is strictly true that there was no Order of the Petite Croix of St Louis, but there *was* an Order of St Louis, open to all Catholic members of the army. Its lowest degree was usually awarded to long-serving junior officers, who were thereby entitled to wear, on a flame-coloured ribbon round the neck, an enamelled gold cross bearing the image of the canonised king. It is clear that Scott's informant was referring to the insignia of a real Order and not the title of a non-existent one. Admittedly that honour had never been conferred on Breck. A record of the nominees for

150

the award of the Order from 1747 to 1792 has survived, as has a central register of the *lettres de nomination* from 1783 to 1791. The Scot's name appears in neither. But he *had* been decorated with the Military Merit Cross, a distinction instituted to reward non-Catholic foreigners with an honour equal in lustre to the Order of St Louis. Furthermore he was in receipt of two known pensions, one from Bouillon's Regiment, the other as a Chevalier in the Military Merit order. And he had at least a forwarding address in the heart of Paris, as the archives show.

If these considerations seem to increase the chances that the meeting really occurred, they must be measured against others which appear to correct the swing – as is so often the case in this complex history. The insignia of his award, for instance, could hardly have been mistaken for those of St Louis. His ribbon was blue and hung from the buttonhole, the other red and suspended round the neck. His gold cross bore on one side a laurel crown with the inscription *Ludovicus XV instituit, 1759*, and on the reverse a sharp-pointed sword with the words *Pro virtute bellica*. The St Louis cross displayed the royal saint. A simple resolution of this conflict of evidence could be that Breck said to Scott's friend and young Ardchattan, 'I was awarded King Louis' medal,' and they, being ignorant of foreign military decorations, assumed it was that of the earlier monarch. The Benedictine garb too is a similarly questionable element. Breck could have lawfully worn it only if he had undergone a conversion to Catholicism followed by a late vocation to holy orders. Father Yves Chaussy, of the Abbaye Sainte-Marie, Paris, a leading authority on monastic life in the seventeenth and eighteenth centuries, generously contributed his knowledge during the preparation of this book. He stated that he had never come across the soldier's name and that it is nowhere mentioned in the *Archives Nationales*. He added that Breck could have changed his name to throw historians off the scent. Or he may have sought refuge in one of the English monasteries or colleges in Paris as a lay brother. That could explain the clerical habit. Dom Geoffrey Scott, OSB, an historian of the Order in the modern period, reveals that there is no trace of an Allan Stewart among English Benedictines. An expert on the Scots colleges and monasteries on the Continent during the era, Father Mark Dilworth, OSB, declares that the man was definitely not ordained at any of them, nor does his name figure in the records of lodgers at those institutions. He adds that he has hit upon cases of false attributions of membership of the Order.

But, by another twist of reasoning, the bogus nature of the old man's credentials enhances rather than reduces the likelihood that he was Allan Breck, for we have proof in plenty that he had no qualms about making baseless claims. The clerical garment might well have been the latest quirk in his infatuation with dress. He may have laid aside his Military Merit Cross for the more publicly recognisable and illustrious one of St Louis, flaunting it with the wistful swagger of an old man-at-arms. Besides, who would dream of staging a complicated charade to pose as a man condemned, by the implication of the trial verdict, as a pitiless killer?

Then there is the question of how much faith to place in Scott's informant, and here we are handicapped by not knowing his identity. His story sounds so calculated to appeal to the great novelist that we are justified in wondering whether he went in for a little fictionalising of his own. Sir Walter himself was of course above totally inventing such an incident, but sometimes he did not examine the facts of an anecdote as closely as their improbable nature deserved, and liked to add an arabesque or two before passing it on to his readers. Nevertheless the weight of testimony comes down heavily in favour of the conclusion that the tale is, in essentials, true.

We catch a late glimpse of Allan Breck in an entry in a notebook whose Englished title is *Alphabetical list of Military Pensioners with Their names and Forenames*:

Stuart d'Artoury (allan) sent to M. Dalliesse (?) Citizen of Paris, rue de la harpe, Hotel de Nassau
26 August 1790

The 'd'Artoury' is a poser. Had he bought a house and a piece of land in the countryside and taken to styling himself like a Scottish laird? A dictionary of ancient French place-names lists no Artoury, nor do modern gazetteers, French or Scots. It sounds suspiciously like an adaptation of Ardtur, an Appin district near which Breck and Ardsheal are known to have skulked after Culloden, and less than a mile as the crow flies from the Portnacroish dram-house where the soldier cried out for the skin of the Red Fox. And who was M. Dalliesse – if that is what the scrawl says? The name bears a distant resemblance to the 'Dardshelle' used by an earlier French clerk to transliterate 'd'Ardsheal'. Is it possible that Breck masqueraded as M. d'Ardsheal, the recipient of M. Stuart d'Artoury's pension? Everything we know of his past suggests that he would not have scrupled at such an imposture. Perhaps the sixty-eight-year old soldier of fortune, one of the last actors in the Appin drama to leave the stage, ended his days a stone's throw from the Seine in that dog-leg street nowadays aromatic from the presence of ethnic restaurants. Cushioned against poverty as he approached a green and no doubt garrulous old age, he may have relished enthralling his hearers with escapades from his gaudy past. Did he ever, one speculates, dwell on the events of 14 May 1752? As for a self-vindicating letter, if he ever wrote one, it has never risen to view. In 1871 the communards joyously set fire to the Hôtel de Ville and the Palais de justice, and 12 000 tomes inclosing eight million Paris records, some dating back to the sixteenth century, went up in smoke. Two-thirds of the city's archives perished. So the historian who sets out to find Allan Breck's plea in rebuttal must face the fact that it may have gone the way of Citizen Kane's Rosebud.

153

10 What the Writers Said

AFTER THE PUBLICATION of the *Supplement* no major
work discussed the trial for more than thirty years. The period
saw the steep and mortal decline of Jacobitism. Prince Charles
Edward lingered until 1788, a sullen and tipsy caricature of the
glittering paladin of yesteryear. None but the most blinkered
sentimentalists who still toasted 'the king over the water' thought
there was the remotest hope of a Stuart restoration. Highlanders
flocked to the colours and fought under the Union Jack in three
continents. As the Jacobite threat evaporated, so too did official
hostility to the families of the attainted lairds. Twenty years
after Glenure's death Ardsheal's relatives occupied all the estate
except the farm at Lettermore and the long-dead laird's mansion.
Lady Ardsheal took up residence on a swathe of Glen Duror that
embraced Aucharn and Auchindarroch. In 1784 the annexed
properties were returned in full to their original owners, and the
lands of Ardsheal were restored to Duncan, the oldest surviving
son of the swordsman of the 'Forty-five. He also assumed the title
of chief of the Stewarts of Appin, Dugald having died without a
male heir. Duncan had emigrated to Connecticut and taken the
post of Collector of Customs. He supported the British in the War
of Independence and was duly rewarded with a collectorship in
Bermuda.

In 1785 there appeared *A Collection and Abridgement of
Celebrated Criminal Trials in Scotland from AD 1536 to 1784*
by Hugo Arnot, an advocate. He criticised the defence team
for entering a plea in bar of trial. That manoeuvre gave the
opposing lawyers leave to make damning allegations which, in
an age of political and tribal bias, might easily have impressed
the jury with the force of sworn testimony. With regard to the
prosecutors, their use of the statements of Margaret and the
children was inhuman and illegal. The evidence against James,
when discussed informally in the drawing-room, was sufficient

154

to make him a suspect but utterly failed to meet the exacting demands of a trial on a capital charge. What few facts there were pointed more directly at Allan Oig than his father. The missing gun, Allan Breck's fear that his foster-brother would give himself away, and Allan Oig's possession of a black jacket were all weighty matters. 'Unless the rule in the scriptures, of visiting the sins of the father upon the children is to be *inverted* by our law, and the sins of the children are to be visited upon the father, I entertain a faint suspicion that a mistake has been committed in the course of this trial, and that (if any of the family was guilty) the prisoner has been hanged instead of his son Allan.'

Commentaries on the Law of Scotland Respecting Crimes by David Hume, the great jurist, were published from 1797 onwards. Of the proceedings against James he remarked: 'It is true, that this trial was attended with some unusual, and indeed censureable circumstances, in the manner of conducting it; but I see no reason to believe that the verdict was not according to the justice of the case, or different from what the jury were warranted to return, on the evidence laid before them.' Hume firmly dismissed the contention that the immediate perpetrator of a crime must be tried before an accessory. On the admissibility of the evidence of relatives he pronounced that there was no absolute rule, as it was necessary to treat each case on its merits. He gave his view that an accessory might be proved guilty 'art and part' of murder if it could be shown that he:

1 dominated the actual killer to an extent that he was no more than an instrument of the instigator's will, or
2 gave assistance after the crime, provided there was evidence that he either incited the offence or had previous knowledge of it.

A short report of the case was included in *A Complete Collection of State Trials*, written by T B Howell between 1809 and 1826. 'The general opinion in Scotland,' he stated, 'seems

155

to be that Campbell was not killed by Allan Breck but by Charles Stewart the pannel's son, who afterwards became a shoemaker in Edinburgh, where he died. It appeared to me that some doubt was entertained in Scotland whether the pannel had any participation in the slaughter.'

In the early 1860s John Dewar made a compilation of folk-tales of Argyll at the request of the eighth duke. Its story of Glenure's death, although decked with yarn-spinners' fictions and contradictions of known facts, must be taken into consideration, supplying as it does an early version passed on in Appin grog-shops, those clearing-houses of muttered confidences. Scots folklorists tend to insist that the old story-tellers presented an accurate central picture, reserving their embroideries for the margins. The tale names Ballachulish's nephew Donald Stewart as the murderer. He had won a shooting competition contested by young men of his patronymic, the first prize being the privilege of gunning down the factor. The runner-up was young Fasnacloich. On the shameful day the two Culloden veterans hid behind a birch tree, resting their guns on a low branch. Donald, nicknamed Molach, which means 'rough' or 'hairy', bore the best musket in Appin. His bullets struck Glenure in the left side and he fell, crying: 'O Mungo! Mungo! Flee as fast as the legs of the horse will permit. I am shot!' When James was sentenced Donald took the decision to give himself up. His friends warned him that Allan Breck's feigning of guilt had failed to save the tacksman, and his own confession would be just as futile. Its only predictable result was a double hanging. Furthermore it would place in the balance the lives of all who were in on the plot. Donald was dissuaded from surrendering himself, but the withdrawal so worked on his mind that he was confined to his bed for a long time. He went off to sea and returned to Appin in old age, dying alone in a herdsman's hut.

On safely touching down in France Allan Breck sent back a letter avowing his guilt and James's innocence. It came too late. Six years later, while fighting as an officer with the French army in Canada, he went by night to the tents of some Argyll men

156

in the enemy camp. He told them he had taken no part in the murder and that his confessional letter was a ploy to absolve his clansmen. He promised to arrange a breach in the circle of troops that then surrounded them, and next night they escaped through the gap.

Some years later the fourth duke of Argyll, a nephew of the trial judge, conducted a progress through his fiefdom. The younger Ballachulish entertained him at his home in lavish style. Gratified, the duke promised him any favour in his gift. Ballachulish asked his permission to get rid of a neighbour whose sight offended him every time he looked out of his windows. Argyll said there was no need to seek his permission to get rid of any neighbour on his own estate. But, replied his host, the neighbour he was referring to was the gibbet on which James Stewart died. The duke told him to put it away quietly, adding that he had argued against its being sited there, and that he had been mortified by the trial, which should never have taken place. From that day on the two clans grew more friendly to each other.

In *The Lord Advocates of Scotland, Vol 2* (1883) George Omond devoted a few paragraphs to the case. His brief biography of Prestongrange acknowledged the man's political services and professional attainments but drew the line at the conduct of the Inveraray trial. 'These proceedings cannot be too strongly condemned,' he thundered. He castigated the Duke of Argyll for persistent bias against the defendant and advanced his own judgment that 'Stewart was sacrificed to political considerations.'

Kidnapped (1886) transformed a rural murder into an adventure yarn that will endure as long as the art of narrative. Stevenson shuffled the facts freely, as he cheerfully admitted, yet the effect of the book was to draw the attention of countless readers to a real, if relatively obscure, *cause célèbre*. The tale appeared during the first great flowering of the detective story, a year before Sherlock Holmes astonished the reading classes in *A Study in Scarlet*. Amateur sleuths pounced on the Appin mystery, a real-life riddle with numerous answers but no solution.

157

They unmasked a far-ranging list of assassins. Allan Breck – now confounded with Stevenson's gallant, self-glorious, loyal, touchy D'Artagnan of the Highlands – was cleared by almost all, in accordance with the stern rule that the leading suspect is never guilty.

Reminiscences of Lord Cockburn, a Lord of Justiciary, were published in 1888 under the title *Circuit Journeys*. He recalled a visit to Ballachulish, the shire's Garden of Eden in his opinion. On putting his foot in a hole he was told that it was the cavity in which the main post supporting James's gibbet was sunk, and it was reverently kept open to mark the position. Cockburn reported that a man once upbraided a Campbell for Argyll's destruction of James. He was jolted by the airy retort that anybody could hang a guilty man, but only the head of Clan Campbell an innocent one. Cockburn's own opinion of the proceedings was stark: '. . . he was unfairly tried. An Argyle and a jury of Campbells . . . sacrificed him because he did not belong to their clan.'

Stevenson's *Catriona* (1893), the master's favourite among his novels, is a sequel to *Kidnapped*. For students of the historical Appin Murder much of its interest lies in the vivid portraits of Prestongrange and James More. The former is presented as a deeply divided personality, a Dr Jekyll kindly to an extravagant extent in private life, ruthless when pursuing his political ends. James More's reptilian qualities are illustrated with a zest that ensured him a deserved place among fiction's great rascals.

The learned and versatile Andrew Lang assigned a chapter of his *Historical Mysteries* to the murder in 1904. The secret of the killer's identity had been handed down, unrevealed to the world, in one Stewart family, he asserted. That name had been spoken to him from two pairs of lips but he was sworn to silence. 'The gist of the secret is merely what one might gather from the report of the trial, that though Allan Breck was concerned in the murder of Campbell of Glenure, he was not alone in it.' The execution of the convicted man, Lang felt, was nothing less than judicial murder.

Three years later *Trial of James Stewart* appeared, edited by David N Mackay. In addition to all the material printed in the 1753 book Mackay appended letters and documents from public and private sources. In 1911 he wrote *The Appin Murder: The Historical Basis of 'Kidnapped' and 'Catriona'*, in which he subjected the case to a more searching examination than it had hitherto received. Allan Breck was a partner in the plot, he decided, but did not fire the shot. The tactics of the investigating force amounted to a catalogue of illegalities framed to rush James to the noose after the palest simulacrum of a trial. The conduct of Argyll, his two colleagues on the bench, Prestongrange, Simon Fraser and the jury was base. Mackay, himself a lawyer, belittled the duke's knowledge of the judicial system and accused him of behaving like a tribal chief. The junior judges knew that the law was being violated but looked the other way. So too did Prestongrange, who should have refused to proceed with the trial after the hearing of evidence, knowing that the proof was insufficient but the packed jury would convict. Fraser's argument that the declarations of Margaret and the children would be produced in evidence, not for the purpose of testing the truth of anything they said, but only as evidence that they had said it, was an astounding piece of casuistry that would have made his father clasp him to his bosom.

In *The Book of Barcaldine* (1936) A Campbell Fraser, a direct descendant of Sheriff Duncan, gave an abbreviated sketch of the matter. Setting much store by local traditional accounts he deduced that young men of leading Stewart families combined and conspired to bring about the assassination. He hazarded the opinion that the murderer was Donald Stewart, but he seems to have confused him with his cousin, young Ballachulish.

In 1939 Duncan C Mactavish, a journalist, studied the archives of Inveraray Castle. His findings were set out in *Inveraray Papers*, three short chapters of which deal with the case. The writer recorded with surprise that he had been unable to find a single document directly connected with the trial. Nevertheless he

159

supplemented existing information with some new and valuable facts. Though obviously at pains to present his findings impartially, Mactavish allowed himself to suggest that James had a personal motive for striving to prevent the evictions, namely the retention of his own sublease in Lettermore. He likewise defended the selection of the jury, citing a precedent indicating that Argyll defendants were tried by assizers from their own shire and Bute men by a panel from theirs. Of James's refusal to attend the corpse he quoted a bizarre explanation that had been submitted to him: the tacksman shared the age-old superstition that a corpse bleeds in the presence of its slayer. The belief was then widespread among the credulous, but it is hardly possible that a man of some learning could have subscribed to it.

The Appin Murder: A summing up by Sir John (later Lord) Cameron was published in *The Scottish Historical Review* in 1954. He scrutinised the trial with a judge's practised eye. The complaint that Argyll ruled out Bute jurors lest they should acquit was groundless, he thought, for it was not known where their sympathies lay. Prestongrange did not deserve criticism, except for creating obstacles for the defence team and admitting the declarations of Margaret and her children. The junior judges were blameless. The disparity between Mungo's description of the fleeing gunman in his precognition and the version he gave in court was highly suspicious. He may have been threatened or cajoled into colouring his courtroom testimony. It was very hard to contend that there was no evidence on which an unbiased jury would have convicted Allan Breck. That James was an accessory before the fact was extremely improbable. 'Red Ewan remains an unattractive and rather sinister figure in the wings, but a distinct "possible".'

Lieutenant-General Sir William MacArthur, who had pursued an interest in the case for many years, set out his views in *The Appin Murder and the Trial of James Stewart* (1960). He had succeeded in exhuming the surviving precognitions, a discovery which threw a new and searching light on some of the murkier

160

corners of the subject. His book, though marred by several minor errors of fact and one major misinterpretation of evidence, is notable for its examination of every aspect of the matter. One of its strengths is the shrewd yoking of apparently unrelated incidents to support the author's case. That case, or cause, was the establishing of the executed man's innocence. The vigorous and readable text crackles with indignation at what Sir William saw as official murder.

Neither James nor his foster-son played any part in the killing, the argument goes, because everything we know of their natures gives it the lie. The older man was a kind-hearted benefactor of widows and orphans, untouched by scandal, incapable of a sudden act of violence in the autumn of his days. Murder was not beyond the scruples of Breck if its rewards were worth the effort, but he would have concocted a scheme that did not condemn him to lurk in the neighbourhood for three days fraught with danger, awaiting a few articles necessary for his flight. James was effectively hanged by a combination of Campbells and the Government, the former motivated by clan vengeance, the latter by reasons of public policy. No blame could be laid to the charge of the Lord Advocate; he was kept in the dark about the intimidation, bribery and illegal stratagems of the private prosecutors, who no doubt handed him a prepared indictment. Argyll acted as the avenger of his clan, and his colleagues on the bench colluded in injustice by refusing to hear the evidence of Airds as to James's good name.

The assassin was probably a Cameron. Glenure had dispossessed some of that clan and was consequently hated by them all. One or more of them, infuriated by what they perceived as tyranny, resolved to close his career. The killer – possibly Serjeant More, MacArthur hints – may have chosen Stewart territory for the deed in order to lead the trail away from his own people.

In 1963 Sir James Fergusson produced *The White Hind and Other Discoveries*, a book of articles on Scottish historical incidents. His survey of the mystery, entitled *The Appin Murder*

Case, sharply rejected criticisms of the prosecutors. We must not view the eighteenth-century Jacobites through the romantic haze cast by Stevenson and Scott, he warned. It was evident that a number of persons took part in the conspiracy. So huge a total of precognitions would not otherwise have been taken by a large team of enquiry officers, who were best placed to know. He set much store by the traditional tale of the shooting-match.

Although drastic steps were taken to make sure that some key witnesses appeared in court James's treatment while under arrest was strictly in accord with the law. The decision to hold the trial at Inveraray was taken solely on grounds of convenience. The printed record of the evidence against the defendants could not convey how conclusive it *sounded* to the court. This impression was expressed in letters by Argyll; John Campbell of Levenside, one of the Crown agents; Prestongrange; Lord Milton; and the Earl of Leven, who was not present but evidently conversed with spectators.

Sir James ventured the guess that the man who fired the shot was Allan Oig, who may have been assisted by one or two others, including John Maccombish the miller. Maccombish also ran the Kentallen Inn. Why he should have figured in the author's gallery of suspects is difficult to understand. He was a tenant due for expulsion, and was one of the party that presented the injunction to Glenure. On the way to the factor's house he was heard by Charles Stewart the notary to brag that he would refuse to budge from his holding. According to the lawyer, when the miller came face to face with Glenure he spoke up 'very impudently'. Maccombish was precognosed and stated that he spent the murder day superintending the transport of ale barrels to Aucharn. At the material time he was serving drinks to John Beg and a woman named Sarah McDonald. Stonefield must have checked this alibi and found it to be true. It seems possible that Sir James confused the miller with another man of the same name, John Maccombish in Ardsheal. He too was a tenant marked down for extrusion. He was twice precognosed, and nothing in his answers indicates that his interrogators had the smallest inkling that he was involved.

Allan Breck was intimately concerned in the arrangements. James was morally innocent but legally guilty. He must have heard something of the plot, yet did nothing to prevent it. This inactivity, coupled with his aid to Breck after the crime, justified his condemnation as being 'art and part'.

11 Conclusions

PLAINLY THE JUDGMENTS we make on the tragedy will be influenced by our preconceptions and the indignation that James's fate must arouse. That he should have been acquitted is the verdict of almost every serious student of the trial. The evidence that sent him to his death was threadbare, even by the none too finicky standards of the period. However, the weakness of the prosecution's case does not prove his innocence. What can the twentieth-century enquirer – 'in the speculations of the closet', as Arnot put it – make of the man's role? Can he set aside natural compassion and ask himself: was he an accessory to the murder? It hardly needs saying that the answer to that question depends on whether the killer was Allan Breck. The only evidence of any substance against the tacksman was that which connected him with the outlaw. In attempting to decide whether James was guilty, therefore, it is essential first to consider the case against Breck.

Look for the motive, says the old rule, and Allan's surname goes a long way to supplying one. His clan hated the Campbells with a passion that was immoderate even among the violent feuds of the time. All Jacobites, and many others, anathematised the tribe for its political pre-eminence and lust for land, but only the Stewarts had, to their own way of thinking, lost their royal dynasty in 1745 through the renegade opposition of the Campbells. In Allan Breck this rage found a focus in Glenure, whose mere assumption of the factorship provoked the growl that he should be shot. After Glenure ejected James from what had been Breck's childhood home he repeatedly threatened him with death. The fact that he issued those menaces when drunk does not mean that they were less than heartfelt, as any toper will confirm. 'Fetch me the Red Fox's skin!' is hard to shrug off as a piece of fuddled braggadocio. The false information that Glenure had tipped off Crawfurd that he was in the area could have been the final straw.

That he fired the shot places no strain on our powers of belief. His threats, his keen interest in Glenure's movements, familiarity with guns and proximity to the site make a list of clear-cut credentials. There was the significant question, overlooked by the prosecution, which he asked Margaret when he took his leave of her on 12 May: had she 'any commands for Rannoch?' This sounds like an absent-minded giveaway of his real intentions, for he was not immediately bound for his mother's country. Perhaps in his mind's eye he already saw himself retreating through that trackless moorland towards an east coast port. Another telling point which was also unaccountably missed by the Crown lawyers was a comment uttered by young Fasnacloich. When Breck left Fasnacloich House on the Monday before the murder the laird asked his son if he had spoken privately to him about the evictions. No, came the reply, and he was glad of it, 'lest the said Allan should do any mischief to Glenure.' Old Fasnacloich reported this in his precognition but was not questioned about it at the trial. The conversation leaves no doubt that his son, Breck's friend, thought him capable of an attack on the factor.

Before leaving Aucharn on his lethal trail the soldier doffed his bright uniform in favour of inconspicuous civvies. Most likely he had by then arranged that a gun should be made available to him in the wood. The single most convincing fact against him is that he enquired of the ferryman if Glenure had yet crossed. We are entitled to assume that Allan knew that Red Colin would be returning that day. Even if he had not heard the news in the course of his visits to Carnoch and Callert he was bound to have been told on arriving at Ballachulish House on Wednesday evening. Hence, his approach to the ferryman looks very much as if it was undertaken to verify that his prey had not passed him by. His whereabouts during the critical hours that followed are a blank, a fact that looks all the more suggestive when one considers that his movements in the preceding week are accurately pinpointed. He did not tell any of the four men to whom we are certain he affirmed his innocence what he was doing at the time of the crime. A guiltless man would surely have protested that he had been at a specific spot, engaged in this or that activity.

The powder-horn he produced when he contacted John Don is an ominous addition. It was not unusual for game-hunters of the period to carry one, but its presence on what was supposed to be a tour of friends takes on a baleful hue; it looks like 'the smoking gun' of detective fiction. The holster he was wearing when seen by the Rannoch innkeeper carries more than a suggestion that he had armed himself with a pistol to resist arrest. The implications of his threat to murder James More must be kept in mind. Granting that the Macgregor's offer to kidnap and bring him to justice gave him ample cause for hostility, one is still struck by his fierce response. The parallel with the Glenure affair is striking. He too was promised retributive assassination, one of his supposed offences being an attempt to bring about Breck's capture.

An obverse view of the events reinforces the case for his guilt. No other serious suspect emerged. The leading Stewarts had unbreakable alibis and the sheriffs decided that Red Ewan was not their man. They obviously ruled out Ballachulish's nephew Donald Stewart in short order. When first examined he was not asked where he was at the decisive moment, so we can take it as certain that Stonefield's preparatory enquiries had already put him in the clear. No other witness is recorded as having been questioned about his alibi. The only 'evidence' against him, the tale first committed to paper a century after his death, must be regretfully classed as fiction. Breck's advertised intention to absolve himself by publishing his story was never carried out. This silence, while Europe resounded with his infamy, is revealingly untypical of a man who made no bones about letting the world know his mind.

If baffled by the balance of evidence we do well to examine the character of the accused. Allan's childhood was disrupted by the death of his father and separation from his mother, which cannot have had a stabilising effect on the boy. As a young man he quickly exhausted his patrimony and ran up debts which James settled, even after Allan had joined the army. The young warrior's instant conversion from Hanoverian to rebel after Prestonpans shows no over-scrupulous adherence to principle. '... a desperat foolish fellow' was the tacksman's curt description of his ward in the papering letter. Yet softer qualities show up in the available data. We see him made welcome wherever he went, and chided by Invernahyle for failing to visit him. He gives a poor man a dram and sets up a delivery of food to him. To the Campbell landlord of the alehouse where he denounced all of the breed he tenders his apologies, offering the charming excuse that it was not himself that was bad company so much as the drink. A sifting of the facts and impressions reveals Allan Breck as shiftless, mendacious and strident, yet courageous and open-handed. The answer to the question 'Was this man capable of murder?' depends to a great extent on the mental make-up of the questioner, but as most people can resort to taking life when pushed beyond the limits of self-control it seems sensible to conclude that Allan was the murderer unless overriding arguments to the contrary can be advanced.

There has been no dearth of ingenious theorists to urge that he was innocent of firing the shot, though most concede that he played a part in the preparations. It is necessary to scan what pleas can be mustered that he was totally without blame. An obvious point in his favour is that dozens of firebrands must have felt like killing the factor, and some of them had access to guns. Dewar related that three assassination squads awaited Glenure, two of them on the Lochaber side of the loch. The tale, if improbable, is not inconceivable, and even if it is untrue it hints at the countrywide hatred felt for the victim. Breck's fulminations, it has been said, were touched off by drink, like his adoptive father's. When sober he never threatened murder. Discussing the evictions with old Fasnacloich, he said that if Glenure had a legal warrant there was no more to be said; if not, he should not be allowed to proceed. We must not lose sight of the fact that only one witness claimed that Allan declared that he would 'dispatch or murder' the factor. This was Robert Stewart, a twenty-year old who drank with him on a night of his April binge. He said that Breck was very drunk at the time, but his own recollection of the conversation may have been cloudy for the same reason. The landlord, who was less likely to be under the influence, quoted Allan as saying that 'he would be fit-sides with Glenure, wherever he met him; and wanted nothing more than to meet him at a convenient place.' The barmaid testified that the drunk said 'that he would not shun Glenure wherever he met him . . .' The point is no trivial one. Breck spoke of *meeting*, not ambushing, the man. He told James that 'he would challenge Ballieveolan, and his sons to fight, wherever he *met* them . . .' It is clear that if he was genuinely bent on homicide he intended to give his adversary a chance to return fire.

Simon Fraser flatly asserted that the scheme was woven when the two defendants met on Monday, 11 May, so Breck's actions from that day forward must be shown to be free of hostile intent. On that morning he told young Fasnacloich that he proposed to leave the country soon, but that he would call back and see him at his home before he left for France. It is difficult to believe that he was telling a pointless lie to a man with whom he was on intimate terms, so we must assume that murder was far from his mind when he set out for Aucharn. The short conversation between Allan and James that afternoon was occupied by the younger man's asking for a loan to ease his passage across the water. James said he was out of cash but could touch William for some in a few days. Allan replied that he had one or two duty visits to make before leaving, but that he would return by the end of the week to collect it. The subject of the evictions may have come up briefly and James outlined his legal moves to stop them. They parted without having had time enough to form the haziest of plans, even if they had wished.

Next day Allan took to the road on his round of courtesy calls.

He left his uniform behind, which he would never have done if he had not meant to come back. His reason for donning James's jacket and trousers was that he hoped to get in a little fishing, a sport in which bright clothes are a drawback. He took along his own powder-horn with the intention of bagging a bird or two if the opportunity presented itself. On Wednesday he headed toward Appin. He had not gone far when he met a certain John Stewart. The time, Stewart said in his precognition, was a little before sunset. Allan told him 'that it was likely he would go to James Stewart's house in Aucharn that night.' Once again it is hard to credit that the soldier was uttering a deliberate lie. He had nothing to gain by telling someone we must presume to be a casual acquaintance that he was going to Aucharn when he intended to stop at Ballachulish House. The straightforward explanation is that when he spoke he had no other destination in mind than James's house – though it should be borne in mind that he said only that he was 'likely' to go there – but he changed his intention, possibly because he was tired. The importance of the point is that it indicates that Allan was not firmly committed to sleeping overnight in Ballachulish, a few minutes' walk from Lettermore Wood.

On the day of the murder he took the notion to loaf around on the stream. With a fishing-rod lent by the herd-lad he began angling near the house. The trout proved shy so he sauntered to a higher station. After a while he remembered that this was the day the factor was due to arrive back. On a sudden whim he made up his mind to have a look at the oppressor he had never seen. It was now about noon, and he wondered if Glenure had already crossed. He went to the south slip and enquired – a venture that would have been the height of folly if he proposed to shoot the man. On being answered in the negative he wandered back to the burn, where the caprice to view the factor soon faded. He whiled away the afternoon idly fishing, sentimentally recalling the days when he and Ardsheal had hidden from Cumberland's men on these very slopes. Then the houses below spilled anxious figures scurrying towards Lettermore. Something momentous was in the air. As a deserter he dared not go down to investigate in case the military were involved. He hid until nightfall, attracted the attention of the maid and gave her his message for Donald. Donald charged him with the slaying and he denied it. He repeated the disclaimer to John Don. To his uncle he declared on oath that he had never seen Glenure 'alive or dead'. Now these were men who, he knew, would never turn him in, and who might not regard the murder as an unmixed tragedy. One or more of them may have taken the stance of Stevenson's fictional Breck that the death of a Campbell was nothing to raise a fuss about. 'They are not so scarce, that I ken!' If the real Allan was the killer his confession could hardly have fallen on more sympathetic ears. Thirty-five years later he was to confront young Ardchattan and swear that he was clean-handed. His decision to write to William was sparked by mounting anxiety. Two days after the shooting he was still within a few miles of the scene, and he had no way of knowing whether Donald had carried his message to James, or if James would respond in the new and precarious situation. Sending John Don to the merchant seemed an imperative course, and we must keep in mind that if he and James had concerted that a money credit should be made available he would not have needed to write a letter.

His comment that James and Allan Oig would be safe if they guarded their tongues was interpreted by Macintosh as an attempt to point the finger away from himself. If the advocate was right we are committed to believing that in order to save himself Breck placed his surrogate family in extreme jeopardy. This in turn implies that he cared nothing for them, but all the existing information negates the presumption. The frequency of his risky visits to Scotland, the fact that he made Aucharn his headquarters, the free-and-easy way he wore their clothes, and his jaunt through the countryside with young Charles all argue a strong attachment to the family. The remark can more plausibly be understood to mean what it visibly implies, that Breck thought

James and his son had taken the law into their own hands. There can be no denying that the soldier was ablaze with rage at Glenure's conduct, but he cannot have been so short-sighted as to overlook the futility of destroying a solitary official. The outrage would bring catastrophe on his clansmen. Perhaps worst of all, it would place in deadly – and, as events proved, fatal – danger the man who had nurtured him.

Mungo Campbell's varying accounts contain nothing that could persuade us that Allan was the culprit. If the young lawyer's precognition is to be believed, the fleeing gunman was wearing dun clothes and was at too great a distance to have pressed the trigger. The man's garments prove beyond question that he was not Breck. Should we accept Mungo's trial testimony that the runaway wore a black jacket we must also take his word that the man was so far away that he would not have known him even if he had seen his face. This is a plain paraphrase of his earlier statement that the bearer of the firelock could not have been the killer. By either variation Breck is cleared of blame, it is contended.

The defence set out above takes for granted that Allan was wholly innocent, but few apologists for the outlaw have taken the position that the only evidence of his guilt boils down to some dram-house bombast and an accidental closeness to the scene of the crime. Most admit that he was up to his ears in the plotting but hold to the belief that he was cast for the part of conspicuous decoy, leading the pursuers away from the real murderer. That theory was first formulated by Crawfurd to Barcaldine as early as eight days after the death, but with the passage of time and accumulation of facts the law agents abandoned it. After initial waverings they never doubted that Allan Breck was the culprit, and their judgment has been reasserted in successive editions of *Burke's Peerage*. The latest issue states without qualification that the factor was 'murdered by Allan Breck Stewart', a verdict with which the writer of this book agrees. The soldier's guilt offers the least dubious answers to the key puzzles of this ravelled mystery.

And if Breck launched the shot was James an accessory? The case against him can be summed up as powerful motive, threats, recent contact with the killer and aid after the fact. The trial evidence brought out several motives. There was the crushing loss of excess rents. There was his supposition that the evictions marked another milestone along Glenure's sacrilegious march to the lairdship of Appin, and the usurper's aggrandisement heralded a corresponding decline in James's control. Perhaps the cruellest blow of all, and the sharpest spur to revenge, was that Glenure drove him from his home. Although he quit when requested, knowing that he could not stave off the move for long, the wrench must have been all the more painful as the interloper was a Campbell. To vacate one's hearth to the hereditary foe without resentment called for a degree of tolerance verging on sainthood. James had a nature capable of exalted forgiveness, as his dying speech demonstrated, but we have Invernahyle's word that he grieved to leave his land. Bitterness, curbed by expedience when he was sober, welled up when drink swept discretion aside. Having decided that Glenure must die he uttered naked hints to his labourers that they should carry out the task, and spoke the quip about helping Campbells to the gallows that may have stung some jurors into retorting in kind. The keeper of an alehouse visited by James on his ride to Edinburgh testified that his customer told him he had challenged Glenure to fight with pistols. Even if this was but a drunken boast it lights up the dark impulses of a mind obsessed. The news of the evictions, with all the difficulties they would bring, could have impelled him to the brink. Deprived of his semi-official authority, his only chance of retaining the prestige he enjoyed with his clansmen was to prevent the removals. His elation on winning the injunction, swiftly dashed by its cancellation, could have pushed him over the edge.

At that moment Allan Breck arrived, as if conjured up by James's blackest urges. He was the perfect blunt instrument, his oft-voiced hatred of the tyrant rivalling that of his guardian.

Ardsheal's taunt that all his friends in Appin must be dead if the despot was allowed to behave as he liked may have prepared his wild spirit for the brutal course James now proposed. It needed only a few minutes' conversation to work out a plan. James would provide the gun, clothes for protective colouring and financial aid to whisk him to safety. Breck's cunning in the heather promised an easy getaway, and at the vital time James would be elsewhere, and seen to be elsewhere. He calculated that Glenure's business in Lochaber would detain him until Thursday, when he would return in the afternoon. As James was low in funds he promised to pick up a sum from William and send it to Caolasnacon, where the murderer would flee after the crime. The soldier left for Glencoe and homed in on the appointed station in the wood three days later. He met an emissary from James who carried the little musket. The two men hid in a bush and Breck shot the factor. The courier, clad in a dun jacket and breeches, seized the gun and fled up the brae, where Mungo saw him vanish behind a ridge. He made his way back to Glen Duror and hid the weapon out of sight of Aucharn, not daring to be seen holding it. That man could have been Allan Oig, but even if he was not, James's son was a party to the conspiracy. It was he who, when the cry went up to hide the arms, pretended that he had tucked the murder gun under cover in the barn.

Meanwhile John Beg had come back from Maryburgh unsupplied. Surprised and alarmed, James sent Sandy Bane next morning, instructing him to ask for the credit as well as cash. By this improvisation Breck would be enabled to write for the money if for some reason it proved impossible to send it to him. The pedlar did as he was bidden, but William and his wife swore otherwise out of loyalty to James. The tacksman was so terrified of Breck's possible capture that he contributed to his escape even after his arrest. If Allan had been caught and forced to confess, the game would have been up. A day later the fugitive was telling the stockman that James and his son would be in no danger if they kept their mouths shut. John Don, like Allan Breck, had grown up in Ardsheal, and owed his job to James's recommendation. It is unimaginable that he invented a quotation that would hammer the final nail in his patron's coffin and brand himself as a loathed ingrate and outcast.

The evidence of Donald Stewart and the servant-girl about meeting Breck on the brae was a trumped-up story to explain away James's knowledge of where to despatch the money. Another lie was the little man's claim that he did not sleep at Aucharn on 11 May. Scarcely less false were his judicial declarations, which made no mention of the missions to Maryburgh of John Beg and Sandy Bane. His wife, daughter and son Charles made statements which were proved beyond contradiction to be fabrications. Allan Oig's denial that he wrote the 'Dear Glen' letter is patently untrue, not only because it contained items of family gossip too intimate and detailed to be faked but also because a forger would have written it in a much more incriminatory vein. In short, James and his adherents threw up a palisade of lies, evasions, threats and bribes that would have saved him but for a determined assault by a numerous and resolute force.

How credible is this assessment? In the present state of our information it is impossible to disprove. Unless further facts are unearthed we cannot confute the theory. Yet close scrutiny discloses its many cracks, and some of the incidents it cites can be shown to bear a diametrically different, and opposing, interpretation.

A cogent argument for James's innocence is that he at all times took proper legal steps to prevent the evictions. He told John More on the day the delegation served the injunction that 'he would support them (the tenants) *as far as Law would allow him* . . .'. This statement, narrated by the labourer in a precognition, was not repeated at the trial, after someone had crossed John More's palm with silver. On the very day of Glenure's death James was still trying to engage a lawyer, having already ensured the attendance of responsible observers for the protest. The charge that the protest was intended as a final bid to block the evictions if the murder attempt should miscarry is hard to sustain in the face of some of his other actions, like his pretence that he slept away from Aucharn and his attempted concealment of the money errands. Would a man who failed to see that the truth about those events was bound to be exposed have had the foresight to stage a fallback strategy?

The crucial courtroom exhibit was the alleged murder gun. It had recently been fired, the prosecution held, but their primitive forensic testimony fell well short of proof. Even if it had been shown that the weapon was discharged not long before it was seized nothing would have been added to the Crown case. John Beg said that it had been used by Breck as recently as March. Young Fasnacloich told Stonefield that Allan Oig had taken it on the shooting expedition to Balnagowan at the end of April or beginning of May. An awkward circumstance from the accusers' point of view was that the musket was in poor condition. Would James have given his henchman a firearm which, in the soldier's own hand, had let him down three times out of four? It is true that an attempt to repair it may have been made six weeks before. Dugald said he saw Breck work on the bigger gun with a file, and the smith summoned by Stonefield to examine the weapons confirmed that it had indeed been filed. It is more than an even bet that Breck turned his hand to the smaller gun at the same time, but it is unlikely that he could have persuaded James that it was now reliable. The practical and influential tacksman would doubtless have borrowed a robust gun from among the several that were known to lie in Stewart hands.

Another thorny question arises: who took the musket back to the glen between its supposed discharge on Thursday and its secretion under the granary-chest by Friday afternoon? Allan Breck did not bring it. If he had, he would certainly have returned James's clothing and collected his own. Allan Oig can be counted out, as his presence in Glen Duror for the whole of the murder day is as certain as any event in the tangled story. The knowledge that neither of these two of James's most likely collaborators returned the gun reduces the chances that he was the instigator. So too does the virtual collapse of the clothes evidence on which the prosecutors so heavily relied. Their contention that a man inciting another to murder lent him his own garments, unaware of, or indifferent to the risk to himself strains credulity. It posits that the schemers made no arrangement for the mutual return of apparel after the crime, although many safe methods suggest themselves. In the three days between the putative forming of the plan and its execution James could have stowed the French uniform in an agreed hiding-place. After the killing Breck could have hurried there and changed clothes, leaving James's to be picked up later. The beauty of this obvious tactic is that it would have given the little conspirator a day or two to rustle up the cash, which he could have placed in the pocket of Allan Breck's outfit. The fugitive could then have collected all he needed at a stroke and fled the district at once.

Colin Maclaren's statement on oath that James said he would take the only course open to him if all legal means failed lacked total conviction in the light of his close association with Glenure's brother. The defence team evidently knew nothing of that relationship, the exploitation of which in cross-examination might have saved the defendant's life. Even as Maclaren's story stands, it has a distinctly counterfeit ring. His oddly clear recapitulation of James's threat gives off an uncertain sound. At the time the alleged threat was uttered James, by his own admission, was so drunk that he could not remember a word of the conversation. How then could Maclaren, who had been drinking along with him, have recalled it so sharply? Must we believe that a seasoned drinker like James had swigged his way to memory loss while his companion, a comparative shaveling of twenty-two, could recreate their talk in mortal detail?

At first glance the borrowing of money looks damaging, yet there are maintainable explanations. In the course of their short chat on the Monday Breck may have asked for cash. James replied that he had none, but would raise a loan. The matter seemed of so little urgency that he allowed nearly three days to elapse before taking action. His failure to state, through the defence advocates, why he needed the money may have been due to fear that an admission that it was intended for the chief suspect would be seen as proof of collusion.

In balancing the arguments for innocence or guilt the condemned man's dying denial must be given its full weight. It takes a good deal of scepticism to dismiss the solemn affirmation of a committed, if wayward, Christian at the point of death. In 1752 the after-life of a man who died swearing lies was eternal suffering. Hellfire was real, not a metaphor for the pain of separation from the Deity, as later, meeker theologians have laid down. If James's final assertion of innocence was a piece of mummery staged to preserve his reputation or shield his family, or both, he had been well instructed on the consequences.

Each of the few pieces of evidence is open to various interpretations, putting it out of the question to give an unarguable yea or nay on the accused's guilt, but James guilty seems more of an assault on common sense than James innocent. He needed no mystic insight to predict that Glenure would be replaced by a harsher factor with a draconian brief, that the evictions would go ahead, and the dead man's clan demand his neck. To believe James guilty we are obliged to accept that a middle-aged, conscientious farmer induced a scapegrace daredevil, a ranter whose mere presence was enough to make him the leading suspect, to shoot a man with whom the ringleader had drunk away the previous Hogmanay. The killer used one of his weapons and wore his clothes. The murder was enacted a few miles from his own doorstep at a spot where he subleased a farm. He waited until the day appointed for the deed before attempting to raise 'run' money. He solicited it, not by a written request to William, as the urgency of the crisis should have dictated, but in a postscript to the letter to Charles Stewart the notary. That letter was a strongly worded entreaty to hasten to Aucharn and represent the tenants next morning – a vital element, we must suppose, in James's contingency plan should the assassination go awry. The writer explained that he had no time to scribble a note to William, and asked the lawyer to relay his appeal for cash. It did not occur to him that Charles might be out of town, which turned out to be the case. As luck would have it, the tacksman had mentioned to his message-bearer, John Beg, that part of his mission was to collect from William payment for the cattle. John Beg called at the shop and learned from the merchant that the lawyer was not at home. William read the letter and refused the loan, professing a lack of funds.

Next morning, in the aftermath of the murder, Donald told James of Allan Breck's request that he should send money to Caolasnacon. We must take in that the plotters had forgotten to settle where it should be delivered, or that perhaps they had, but Breck thought it prudent to send his partner a reminder in case it had slipped his memory. Sandy Bane was enlisted to make the new approach. He was directed to ask not only for cash but a five-pound credit for John Don. Why James waited until the day after the crime to fix up a credit he had promised Breck four days earlier defies analysis. He could have entrusted that duty to John Beg on the previous day. There was another instruction: he was to tell William to let Cameron of Glen Nevis know that the horse he had ordered was now ready for collection. Even while tidying up the loose ends of his savage project James remained enough of a businessman to clinch a deal. Sandy returned from Maryburgh with three guineas but he had inexplicably refrained from asking for the cash credit, according to the stories of William and his wife, although he had three opportunities for doing so. On the first occasion, when he entered the shop, he may have held his peace because there were customers present, but when he met the couple separately and alone next day he was equally silent on the subject. Nor did he allude to the credit in his judicial declarations of 4 and 30 June. Nor did Crawfurd refer to it in a letter dated 29 June, when he wrote: 'Alexr. Stewart was sent by James Steuart of Aharn to Fort William, to get this £5 from William Steuart . . .'

Summarised thus, the case against James crumbles. Quite apart from the inadequacy of the evidence his character and way of life form a compelling plea in his favour. He was a hustling man of affairs, a type less common in these days of public enterprise and specialisation, but there are still enough about to fix their qualities. Chief among these is self-confidence. James sounded the true note when he told his labourers that it was people like them who would suffer the iniquities of Red Colin, whereas he could always shift for himself. There is no reason to doubt him: when the factor moved him out of Auchindarroch he contrived to rent an adjacent property from a Campbell. His dismissal from the unofficial post of subfactor did not involve any financial loss, and the impending evictions would set him back only the few pounds of annual rent on his sublet farm. Another distinguishing mark of the species is a capacity for, and relish in, organisation. A smoothly engineered operation gives them a sense of fulfilment that has little to do with a swelling bank balance. If James, whose business talents were acknowledged even by his political foes, had planned the enterprise he would have run it efficiently. He would not have chosen his foster-son as his implement or allowed three days to pass before laying his hands on the modest sum that stood between himself and the hangman. The assassin would never have worn his clothes or used a musket from his household. To sum up, James had very little to gain and everything to lose by doing away with the factor, and if he had set his hand to it there would not have been the resulting shambles.

To decide on his innocence or guilt is a choice between two narratives riddled with implausibilities. On those unsatisfactory terms the modern sleuth is forced to conclude that it is marginally more likely that the tacksman had nothing to do with the murder. How far he was to blame by his inflammatory outbursts for creating the climate in which Glenure's death was 'on' is a question for the moralists. But can the latter-day student of this perplexing case construct a cohesive theory that resolves its contradictions? The present writer offers his own ensuing conjectures which, he believes, provide the most rational answers.

The two Allans, Breck and Oig, finalised plans for the murder in the afternoon and evening of Monday, 11 May. We know from Allan Oig's first judicial declaration that they discussed the evictions in the afternoon. Breck agreed to do the shooting. The plotters paid a surreptitious visit to the barn and checked the small musket. Reluctantly they took the decision to use it; to borrow a fitter weapon would increase the chances of exposure dangerously, and if the assassination should literally misfire Breck would surely escape, consoled by a determined if vain endeavour. They applied their minds to the questions of where and when. Glenure must return before Friday, the term day of the leases. His business in Lochaber consisted mainly of obtaining a removal order against certain tenants in Mamore, evicting them, and collecting rents from other leaseholders while settling their terms of tenure for the coming year. Those duties could not be completed in less than three days, so it could be predicted with some confidence that he would come back on Thursday, possibly at a later hour. The fact that Glenure had the added problem of resolving the ferry dispute with the people of North Ballachulish, which Allan Oig had learned about from the laird, strongly indicated that he would make that settlement his last stopping-place before crossing to Appin. He would doubtless take the quickest route, by ferry. Hence the 'where' of the ambush needed no debate. Lettermore Wood, with its abundance of cover, was tailor-made. If their target should choose to take a boat across the loch from Onich to Kentallen, as he had done once before, the enterprise would have to be deferred. Though Breck could have made his way from Lettermore to Kentallen in the time it would take an oarsman to make the crossing, he could hardly hope to shoot Glenure in the few yards between the landing-pier and the inn.

Breck said he could not leave Scotland without calling on

Ardsheal's sisters. He would spend the next two days at Carnoch and Callert before turning back to stay at Ballachulish House on Wednesday night. By mid-morning on Thursday he would be in place in the wood. He said he needed money and asked Allan Oig if he had any. No, was the reply, nor had his father. He would prevail on James to raise a loan which would be sent to the marksman along with the gun. The foster-brothers spent some hours working out the other details of their scheme.

On the following morning the prospective killer started out for Ballachulish. He wore James's garb for greater anonymity, regretfully abandoning his French outfit. To carry it with him might create inconveniences at a time when he must concentrate single-mindedly on the essential business. In the pocket of his jacket he carried lead bullets and a flat powder-horn, both items given him by Allan Oig, who had acquired the powder-horn secretly, and by using it, and not one from his own home, was minimising the risk to himself. If the attempt should fail and the horn fall into official hands it could not be traced to Aucharn.

At some time on that day, Tuesday, Allan Oig briefed the third member of his team. His identity is a matter of guesswork, but two 'possibles' are worth a mention. One is the Donald Macdonald who, it may be recalled, arrived at Aucharn on the afternoon of the Monday preceding the murder. He must have stayed at or near the house overnight, as he accompanied Allan Oig and Archibald Cameron to the island of Balnagowan twenty-four hours later. He walked back to Glen Duror with James's son and disappeared from the records at that point. If he made a precognition it has not lasted, and his name was not included in the preliminary list of about 250 persons who might be called as witnesses. His age could be estimated as in the mid to late teens, for John Beg, who was twenty-seven, described him as 'a young lad'. His known contact with the two Allans at a decisive moment places a questionmark against his name. If he conspired to kill the Campbell it is hard to ascribe a motive, unless it could have been belated revenge for the massacre at Glencoe sixty years previously, when his great-grandfather was among the first to be slaughtered.

The other candidate for the part of third murderer is Archibald Cameron. In his precognition he said he saw Breck at Fasnacloich House on the Monday morning. It is more than a real possibility, therefore, that he had slept there on the preceding night and discussed the evictions with him. In the afternoon he walked to Aucharn, supped with the family, shared a bed with Allan Oig and went to Balnagowan after lunch with his bedfellow and Macdonald. Nothing is known of the conversation of the excursionists. Cameron left the others in order to spend the night at his aunt's in Cuil. In his precognition he made no reference to the island trip, conveying the impression that he walked straight from Aucharn to Cuil. On the next day, Wednesday, he made his way to Lagnaha, where he slept the night. He said that at about noon on Thursday he went to Inshaig and stayed there until he heard that Glenure was dead. It is most likely that he spent this time at the dram-house, whose landlord was closely related to him, although he did not say so. If he drank the hours away he must have been there when Allan Oig, Charles, their sister Elizabeth and her friend Mary Stewart turned up in the late afternoon, yet neither of James's sons alluded to his presence in their declarations. Cameron was listed as a witness by both prosecution and defence, but spoke for the prosecutors. His evidence, particularly his statement that he did not see James and Breck speak privately on the evening of 11 May, was pointedly favourable to the accused.

Apart from the fact that both these young men met the main schemers shortly before the murder and that there are dubious but explicable lacunae in Cameron's story, no grain of positive evidence against them exists in the documents. The lawmen must have vetted their alibis minutely and consigned them to the 'eliminated from our enquiries' category. It is much more to be surmised that Allan Oig's recruit was a man from his own district, one he had already sounded out. There cannot have been great difficulty in finding a willing hothead in a population seething with resentment. Since he is an unknown quantity it may be convenient to call him X. Allan Oig spelled out the plan. On the following night he would secretly take the smaller musket from the barn and meet him at an agreed location not far from Aucharn. He would give him a sum of money for Breck. They would find a secure hiding-place and install the gun there. Next morning X was to pick it up, taking every precaution against being observed, and carry it and the cash to the sniper by unfrequented ways. He must stay with Breck until the deed was done, bring the musket back to the glen and restore it to the hide, where Allan Oig would recover it when darkness fell. It was vital that the gun be taken back to the barn, he instilled. In the inevitable hue and cry the hunters might learn of its existence, and if it was missing they would make the obvious deduction. X must protect himself with an alibi that would stand up to a scrutiny of the most exhaustive kind.

On the same Tuesday young Allan asked his father to send John Beg next day for a loan to smooth Breck's journey to France. If Glenure were to arrive back in Appin with a military escort, he pointed out, the deserter's life would be at hazard. James grudgingly assented. On that day too the factor sent his message to the landlord of the Kentallen Inn announcing that he would dine there on Thursday evening. By the next morning Allan Oig had learned that the attack could be carried out on the morrow, as he had anticipated. He asked his father if he had sent John Beg for the cash. No, came the response, as the rascal had not yet come back from his mission to old Alexander Stewart the notary.

By the time darkness fell John Beg had not returned. Allan Oig took the gun to his meeting with X. He told him he had not yet got hold of the money but would have it by the next evening. X must tell Breck that he, Allan Oig, would bring the loan to him at any refuge he chose. He would also take the opportunity to carry along his prized clothes. Breck could expect him at the earliest moment he could slip away without arousing suspicion. The conspirators arranged to meet on the following night at the same spot in order that Allan Oig could repossess the musket and learn where to take the necessaries. They then concealed the firearm in a safe cranny and parted.

John Beg spent that Wednesday at the lawyer's house, waiting for him to come back from his fishing trip. It was eight o'clock in the evening before the veteran angler put in an appearance. He read James's letter and wrote a reply that he was too fatigued to represent him at the evictions. He warned John Beg to make sure that he reached Aucharn by dawn so that his master should have enough time to engage another lawyer. The envoy delivered the letter to James at an early hour on Thursday morning. He in turn wrote his appeal to Charles Stewart, requesting him in a postscript to ask William for a loan, and the durable John Beg took off for Maryburgh.

A few hours later X, dressed in a dun jacket and breeches, took the weapon and threaded his way undetected to the wood. He made a successful rendezvous with Breck and told him of the cash problem. The gunman nominated the goat-house on the brae above Ballachulish House as his place of retreat. He primed the musket and selected his firing position behind a leafy bush a few yards above the woodland path. X crouched in a similar nook a little higher on the hillside for swifter escape. Together they waited, eyes trained on the opposite shore of the loch where the road from Onich to North Ballachulish hugged the water-line. As time wore on Allan Breck wondered if the factor had already gone by. Deciding that the danger in asking the ferryman was negligible since everyone in Appin was absorbed in Glenure's movements, he walked to the slip. Reassured, he returned. Five hours later he was ready when Red Colin's horse passed, slowly negotiating the tree-roots that traversed the path. As soon as he pressed the trigger Allan tossed the musket to X. Both men lit out up the hill, Breck at an angle that would take him back to Ballachulish, X in the opposite direction towards Glen Duror.

So smooth was the hand-over and so abrupt X's flight that he speedily covered a lengthy stretch of hillside. As he neared a convenient ridge he risked a backward glance and took in the horrified gaze of Mungo Campbell. He spurted over the rise, traced a circuitous route to the glen and inserted the gun in its hiding-place.

Allan Oig meanwhile furnished himself with a solid alibi. In the morning he established his presence up the glen by warning two women to keep their cattle off his father's land, and in the afternoon he stayed visible to several pairs of eyes. He was told of the murder on returning from Inshaig. Then came the bad news: William had refused the loan. His clandestine journey to deliver the cash would have to be postponed, delaying Breck's escape and thereby shortening the odds against his own detection. He beseeched his father to try again and James consented, needing no compulsion in the new and dangerous state of affairs. The tacksman told Margaret and Allan Oig to order the labourers to thrust the weapons into the thatch. If this instruction came as an unexpected crisis for his son he handled the moment coolly by telling John Beg and Dugald that he had already hidden the little musket under the girnel. When it grew dark he left the house for the appointment with his confederate. They uncovered the gun and X reported that Breck was holed up at the goat-house. Allan Oig took the firearm home and furtively placed it beneath the girnel. Next afternoon he suggested to his father that it would be safer to relocate the arms out of doors. James concurred and ordered the Maccolls to do so. By this device Allan Oig certified that the gun was found where he had said he hid it on the evening of the murder.

Allan Breck fled to the goat-house, stopping only to pick up the greatcoat he had left on the bank of the burn. He watched the Ballachulish Stewarts stream towards Lettermore and may have seen the laird walk back 'trembling and wringing his hands', as his housekeeper depicted him. In growing apprehension – 'greatly frightened' is the stockman's description of Breck's demeanour when they met two days later – his thoughts flew to Aucharn. Had James guessed he was the killer? Would the shrewd tacksman calculate that Allan Oig's plea for money meant that his son was in the plot? The fact that the lad patently knew where to send it would need a tenable explanation. Had X got back to tell Allan Oig where he had taken cover? He might have run into a stray redcoat patrol. If he did not manage to reach young Allan his foster-brother would not know where to bring the cash. The panicking Breck determined to apply directly to James. His second father would not fail to respond, and the despatch of money could not place him at risk if the transaction should ever stand revealed, for he could justly plead a parental impulse towards a man who was not known to have committed a crime. At dusk he succeeded in attracting the notice of the housemaid. His first two questions drew the information that Glenure was dead and that she did not know who the killer was. He asked her to tell Donald to go to James and beg him to send the money. The fact that he did not specify where to send it meant only that he intended to lurk near the goat-house until it arrived. On obtaining her promise to convey the message he concealed himself again. He now knew that his alehouse blusterings had been converted to bloody reality. He had shot a helpless civilian in the back, an act which would strike his regimental comrades as a blasphemy against the rough code of the soldier. To admit his guilt was forever impossible.

The housemaid dutifully and accurately told Donald of Breck's appeal. Donald's conflicting version of their conversation stemmed from his faulty recollection of the melodramatic exchange. A few hours previously he had assisted in carrying the corpse to the water's edge. Now he was to have a tense encounter with the man he believed to be the slayer. In such conditions honest misunderstandings are inevitable. He rushed out and accused the murderer point-blank. Allan denied it. Donald told him in coarse monosyllables to take himself off from the neighbourhood, as his presence was imperilling the

Ballachulish family. Only if he retired to another hideout, he added, would he carry the message. After a moment's thought Breck chose Caolasnacon, with its woody sanctuary in the Corrynakiegh gully. The place had the tactical advantage that John Don lived there. Should there be any delay in receiving the necessities the stockman could always be sent to Maryburgh. Donald relayed Breck's appeal to James next morning. The worried tacksman persuaded Sandy Bane to approach William, but said nothing of a cash credit. Throughout the pedlar's long months of imprisonment he stuck resolutely to the truth. When the prosecutors learned during the plea in bar of trial that Donald and the maid would testify that they had spoken to Breck on the brae their case looked bankrupt. That night Sandy was coerced by the jailer's traditional arsenal of threats, lies and inducements. The defection of some of James's other friends may have helped to drive him to perjury. Next day he swore the lie about the credit. It was economically tailored to 'prove' that James and Allan Breck, while out of touch, took predetermined and co-ordinated steps to transfer the money.

The decision to send the French rig-out was contrived by Allan Oig. James confided to his wife and older children that he had been appealed to by Breck. His son worked on him to include the clothes and he agreed. When faced with being interrogated Margaret, Charles and his sister Elizabeth were in a cleft stick. To admit that the soldier left Aucharn in James's costume would hand the pursuers an item of evidence that could be gravely misconstrued. Moreover it would leave them tongue-tied in the face of the foreseeable riposte: 'We know that he came to your home in his uniform. If he departed in another garb, as you say, please produce the uniform.' If they were to say that he wore the uniform they risked being proved liars by witnesses who saw Breck after he left Aucharn. Comforted by the belief that their judicial declarations could not in any case be used against James in a courtroom they opted for the second, disastrous alternative.

Donald and the servant-maid said nothing in their precognitions of the twilight encounters with Allan Breck, having been warned by Ballachulish and his son not to divulge that James was in contact with the fugitive after the murder. When Edinglassie arrived he insisted that they tell the full story in court. He explained that the indictment revealed that the evidence of Sandy Bane and John Don would bring to notice the post-murder link between the co-defendants. It was therefore now a matter of life and death to show that the link was forged *after* the murder, and that it was Breck who made the connection.

John Don, though dedicated to saving his own hide, and not above lying to achieve it, nevertheless swore the truth. His inconsistent stories were the wrigglings of a man placed in the fearful predicament of having to protect his brother Red Ewan, his friends and himself. The threat that he might be charged as an accessory after the fact broke his resistance. His deadly testimony that Allan Breck told him James and his son would come to no harm if they guarded their words was genuine. What Allan meant by the statement was not what the jurymen read into it. He was implying:

1 that Allan Oig, by a verbal blunder, could hang himself, and
2 that James might inadvertently betray his son by letting slip what he suspected.

The jury inferred that they shared the same guilty secret and were equally culpable.

Mungo was the sole witness of whom it can be affirmed without reservation that he swore falsely. The man he saw fleeing the scene in a dun coat and breeches was of course X. He was too far away to have fired the shot, said Mungo's precognition. In court he averred that the runner wore a short dark coat. It is significant that he did not mention the man's nether garment which, to an observer looking up a steep hillside, must have been much more visible than the coat. He could not quite bring himself to say that a pair of dun breeches, a short covering tied below the knee, was a pair of long blue trousers. Perhaps he felt that if the whole truth should some day emerge, the fewer lies he would have to explain away the better. He swore that the man was at such a distance as to be unrecognisable, but he carefully omitted his earlier opinion that he could not have pulled the trigger. Thirteen witnesses were questioned about the clothes Breck wore at the time of the crime. The garments were exhibited in court and at least two men were asked to identify them. Mungo, the eyewitness of the presumptive murderer, was not. The prosecuting lawyers, who had seen his precognition, chose to spare a colleague the embarrassment of perjuring himself twice.

The foregoing explanation is but one of many for the events surrounding the tragedy. It is clearly impossible to prove, but to its author it seems to fit the facts and characters more convincingly than other theories. Some of the details could be replaced by well-grounded alternatives without affecting the central thesis. The powder-horn, for instance, may have been brought from France by Breck with a view to shooting a few birds with his friends. He left it in James's pocket in case he should be captured with the accusatory article. Allan Oig could have talked X into undertaking to deliver the cash and clothes to Breck at the goat-house, a mission abandoned due to the turn of circumstances. He could have reasoned that he himself dared not tackle the task; as a front-line suspect his movements were bound to be subjected to intense examination.

The murder – or two murders, as some insist – is almost forgotten in the green glens where the melancholy story ran its course. To those who like to draw broad conclusions from particular occurrences the affair offers a rich choice. They may sigh again over the corrupting nature of power, for it was the dominance of Clan Campbell that lured several members to their transgressions. Connoisseurs of nemesis can smile to note that the prosecutors published the book of the trial to demonstrate the rightness of their cause. Official lawlessness paraded itself in the persons of the judges and Lord Advocate, all of whom turned a blind eye to breaches of the system they were appointed to uphold and whose sacred character they hymned. Prestongrange in particular deserves censure. He had read Mungo's precognition, with its description of the absconding gunman, before drawing up the indictment. Someone – Barcaldine? – passed him the whisper that the young lawyer intended to change his story, so he made no reference to the runaway. Stevenson got it right when he made his Prestongrange admit that he was acting as a politician and not a dispenser of justice. The Advocate's handling of the case was a conclusive argument for the separation of powers. Whether Mungo's motive in swearing away a man's life was revenge or self-advancement, his actions supply ammunition to those who believe that to the legal mind truth is that which can be successfully maintained in court. The futility of violence was exposed for the millionth time by the fact that the tenants, excepting the Lettermore widow, were evicted, and wide Stewart acres passed into the hands of strangers. Opponents of capital punishment quoted the case to some effect as an endorsement of their struggle. Temperance reformers pointed to a man whose thirsty tongue had talked him to his execution. Public disgust at the composition of the jury led to legal changes.

One of the most striking impressions of the trial is the truthfulness of the ordinary people involved. Time and again a testifier was asked a question to which only he knew the answer, and time after time his reply ran counter to his natural sympathies. It could even be argued that the lies of James's family were framed to prevent a fatal distortion of the truth. Several individuals in the sombre tale attract our respect. Donald Campbell of Airds shines through as a staunch friend of the accused, frustrated in his efforts to help. The two Ballachulishes, and especially the son, behaved nobly. Stonefield commands praise for his fairness and professionalism, though his scolding of James beneath the gibbet is past forgiveness. Impressive too is the busy competence of Edinglassie who, if he really was *By-stander*, missed his true vocation as a pamphleteer.

To the researcher who lives on a planet a button's touch away from incineration the shooting of a minor official shrinks to the status of a misdemeanour. Close study, however, makes it easier to understand the horror it aroused. He is wafted back to a world that still holds something of its pristine freshness. He watches the nomadic young Jacobites stroll through Arcadian landscapes from one clansman's dwelling to another, sure of a welcoming board and bed. Fading Campbell letters are replete with the very stuff of living – new babies, condolences, fireside accidents, purchases, excuses for not writing, deaths, disappointments, small triumphs. They evoke a warm and supportive community, a family indefinitely extended and unified by the ties of a common ancestry and a shared name. Yet it was this consuming loyalty, carried beyond the bounds of reason, that brought Red Colin and James to their ignominious deaths. Inter-tribal hatred, the ugly underside of the fabric, drove Allan Breck to the savage act. This violent aspect of the clan ethos was one of the considerations that had provoked the Government to stamp out the ancient social structure, and its efforts were attended with such success that the mystique of the clan chiefs had dissolved, reducing them to mere landowners. The murder of Glenure no doubt served to convince traditionalists that Scotland had outgrown its old forms of organisation. It might not be stretching the facts too far to say that the clan system expired in the wood of Lettermore, not with a whimper but a bang, on that spring afternoon.

BIBLIOGRAPHY

MANUSCRIPT SOURCES

Scottish Record Office, HM General Register House, Edinburgh
West Circuit Book Beginning 21 September, 1752. JC 13. 10
Forfeited Estates 1745. Minutes of Barons of Exchequer Vol. 1
    1747 54. E700
Forfeited Estates 1745. Correspondence. Barons of Exchequer
    and Treasury 1751–56 Vol. 2. E702
The Bighouse Papers GD87/1/42 50
John MacGregor Collection GD50
Campbell of Stonefield MSS GD14 Nos. 138, 139
Campbell of Barcaldine MSS GD170 Nos. 1038/1/1–2, 1129,
    1206, 1313
Dewar MSS RH/1/2/566/2

National Library of Scotland, Edinburgh
Precognitions, Appin Murder, Adv. MS 25.3.10
MS Records of the Barons of Exchequer in Scotland. Letters
    Relating to Forfeitures, Vol. 1, Adv. MS 28.1.6
Erskine Murray Correspondence 1752–3 MS 5077 pp 35,
    37, 46
Walter Blaikie Collection MS 295, 315

Court of the Lord Lyon, Edinburgh
Campbell MSS

Public Record Office, Chancery Lane, London
State Papers, Scotland, Series 2, SP 54, Vol. 42

Public Record Office, Kew Gardens
Treasury Minute Book Apr 1747 – Dec 1751 T29.31
Treasury Minute Book Dec 1751 – Dec 1757 T29.32

The British Library, British Museum
Add. MSS 32,727 pp 276, 287–8, 290, 406–7; Add. MSS
  32, 728 p 92; Add. MSS 32,730 p 38; Add. MSS 32,753 p 55;
  Add. MSS 35,447 pp 217, 235, 252, 269–70, 282–3,
  286–9, 295–6, 299, 301, 309; Add. MSS 35,450
  pp 211–12, 223–5, 229–30

Service Historique de l'Armée de Terre, Château de Vincennes
Inspections 1776 à 1778. YA 176 Serie A
Pensions de Réforme. YA 190
Repertoire alphabetique des Pensionnaires militaires, etc., YA
  195
O'Gilvy, écossais, 2e registre. IYc 637

BOOKS

Trial of James Stewart in Aucharn in Duror of Appin (Hamilton
  and Balfour, Edinburgh, 1753)
Supplement to the Trial of James Stewart by a By-stander
  (London, 1753)
*A Collection and Abridgement of Celebrated Criminal Trials
  in Scotland from AD 1536 to 1784 by Hugo Arnot, 1785*
Commentaries on the Law of Scotland respecting Crimes by
  David Hume (Edinburgh, 1819)
A Complete Collection of State Trials by T B Howell (1809–
  1826)
The Lord Advocates of Scotland, Vol. 2 by George Omond
  (David Douglas, 1883)
Kidnapped by R L Stevenson (Cassell and Co., 1886)
Circuit Journeys by Lord Cockburn (David Douglas, 1888)
Catriona by R L Stevenson (Cassell and Co., 1893)
Pickle the Spy by Andrew Lang (Longman, Green and Co.,
  1897)
Historical Mysteries by Andrew Lang (Smith, Elder, 1904)

193

Trial of James Stewart edited by David N Mackay (Notable Scottish Trials Series, 1907. Notable British Trials Series, 1931)

Scottish Forfeited Estates Papers, 1715; 1745 by A H Millar (Scottish History Society, 1909)

The Appin Murder: The Historical Basis of 'Kidnapped' and 'Catriona' by David N Mackay (William Hodge and Co., 1911)

Robert Louis Stevenson and the Scottish Highlanders by David B Morris (Observer Press, 1929)

The Book of Barcaldine: three centuries in the West Highlands by A Campbell Fraser (Alexander Maclehose and Co., 1936)

Inveraray Papers by Duncan C Mactavish (Oban Times Ltd., 1939)

Argyll in the Forty-five by Sir James Fergusson (Faber and Faber, 1951)

The Appin Murder and the Trial of James Stewart by Sir William MacArthur (JMP Publishing Services, 1960)

The White Hind and Other Discoveries by Sir James Fergusson (Faber and Faber, 1963)

Inveraray and the Dukes of Argyll by Ian G Lindsay and Mary Cosh (Edinburgh University Press, 1973)

Argyll: The Enduring Heartland by Marion Campbell (Turnstone Books, 1977)

Jacobite Estates of the Forty-five by Annette M Smith (John Donald Publishers, Edinburgh, 1982)